THE BRIDPORT PRIZE
POETRY AND SHORT STORIES

JUDGES
Alexis Lykiard • Short stories
Selima Hill • Poetry

redcliffe

First published in 1995 by
SANSOM & COMPANY
an imprint of Redcliffe Press Ltd, Bristol
for Bridport Arts Centre,
South Street, Bridport, Dorset

© the contributors

ISBN 1 872971 44 X

British Cataloguing-in-Publication Data.
A catalogue record for this book is available from the British Library.

All rights reserved. No part of this publication may be reproduced, stored in a retrieval system, or transmitted, in any form or by any means, electronic, mechanical, photocopying, recording or otherwise, without the prior permission of the publishers.

Typeset by Mayhew Typesetting, Rhayader, Powys and printed by The Longdunn Press Ltd, Bristol.

Contents

Story Report *Alexis Lykiard*	5
Poetry Report *Selima Hill*	10
Watching Men on the Moon *Richard Griffiths*	14
The Blessed Hieronymus *Peter Regent*	23
Take the 'A' Train *D.A. Callard*	32
The Fan *Alex Barr*	47
Change at Crewe *William Campbell*	60
Lifesaving *J.L. Brooke*	71
School Rules *Nicola Waldron*	75
Sun-Patch *George Hobson*	76
The First Tourist Sends Out Two Thousand Questionnaires *Kearan Williams*	78
The Dying-Room *John Gurney*	80
Strip-Wash *Frances Angela*	82
Roots *William Scammell*	83
Two Dreamings *John Dick*	84
Sandman *Sheenagh Pugh*	85
Cows *Alison Spritzler-Rose*	87
The Call-In *Stephen Duncan*	88
Under the Blue-Printed Sky *Adam Schwartzman*	90
Gone Fishing *Tanya Winter*	91
Frank's old Mansion *Phil Bowen*	92
Songs of Praise *Brian McManus*	94
Earth-Stars *Sylvia Oldroyd*	95
Casualty *Jo Pestel*	96
The Open Mouth *Sarah Carr*	98
The Time Machine *David Almond*	100
The Last Time We Talked *Ron Smith*	113
The Gold of Tolosa *Blánaid McKinney*	126

Off *David Brown* 135
On the Edge *Kevin Parry* 142
The Death of the Author *John Wakeman* 154
Biographies 164

ALEXIS LYKIARD

Story Report

This year just on three and a half thousand stories, from all over the world, were entered for the competition. During the months I spent reading them all, I made a list of the most popular subjects – or anyhow those ingredients which seemed most liable to recur. There was (compared to my previous stint as a judge, in 1989), a disproportionate amount of fictional death and disaster: very young and very old people died most frequently, it appeared, via accidents, abortion, euthanasia, AIDS, anorexia, bulimia, addictions and a whole range of terminal illnesses. This was apart from fatalities in the two World Wars (especially in the Holocaust), in Bosnia and in Northern Ireland. Much hospital visiting took place, of course, and there was childbirth and child abuse, adoption and abduction, blackmail, murder and much rape, some of males. Funerals abounded. The inner cities were collapsing, and politicians (usually right-wing) were exposed in scandals. Even darker or odder themes resurfaced in the science fiction and weird genre tales: vampires, cannibalism, reincarnation, crop circles, assorted aliens, diabolical pacts, spooks and mutants. On the more mundane front, schooldays, divorce, legacies and retirement were greatly favoured, if not overworked, themes, and numerous stories dealt with animal rights, foxhunting, dogs and cats . . .

I was finally persuaded that, as a rule, topicality alone led merely to overstatement or banality. Too many stories were incomplete jottings, anecdotal fragments, static things – rather than vital microcosms, small fictional worlds possessing a fully-realised original dramatic life of their own. Unsuccessful works often ended, predictably, in tears or laughter: either way, a rather stale technical device would invariably fail to deliver a satisfying, creatively inevitable conclusion. But a story which genuinely moves readers or makes them laugh is a rare and hard won achievement. Such stories *show*, they don't *tell* – and thus they linger in the mind. Because, too, their authors' use of words is accurate, imaginative, precise, the stories demand (and improve on) re-readings. Granted you have to pan for such gold with patience, but it shines out all the more clearly when discovered amid piles of dross.

But clearing, and dispensing with, the dross has to be done first, before the prizes can glitter. Put another way, this means: the bad news first. It was obvious, even more than six years ago, that would-be winners aren't reading much; whereas would-be *writers* always do, and so they should! Reading voraciously and well is a vital part of learning the short story craft. Ignorance of what excellent work has been and is being done, leads to writing in stilted, conventional and lifeless modes. It was also clear that educational standards have undergone a marked decline: poor spelling, awkward or misleading grammar and punctuation, inconsistencies, clichés and repetitions were more in evidence than I recalled or could have wished. And yet, there at the back of one's mind, murmurs that master storyteller William Saroyan: '. . . I am not especially concerned about words as words. I care about them *enough*, of course, but what I am really after is what I can get them to mean, apart from themselves, or even in spite of themselves.' What I have called dross is inert, has no gleam, reflects nothing. Good writers are never careless and relish words, situations, people: they show us something of value.

So I was delighted to find what are, in my view, an exceptionally fine group of nuggets – sixteen highly readable and accomplished stories I should think any editor would be proud to publish. Heading the list is WATCHING MEN ON THE MOON, a subtle, poignant and economical story by Richard Griffiths (third prizewinner last year). Here the central image is wonderfully apt and sustains a moving story of failed relationships and larger human aspirations. One critic wrote that the late Raymond Carver 'must be the first creative writer to do full justice to the role of TV in domestic crises'. Griffiths, a writer to watch, does it here – and more – quite superbly.

THE BLESSED HIERONYMUS by Peter Regent wins second prize for its quirky humour and originality. There was very little humour around this year, very little that worked, anyhow, and Regent's wittily satirical fable about sin, sanctity, dubious gurus and the even more doubtful certainties of dogma seemed especially appropriate as we move towards the millennium. Delightfully offbeat, and like nothing else in the competition this year.

D.A. Callard's TAKE THE 'A' TRAIN, could also be described as delightfully offbeat, and is, to my own particular great pleasure, that rare thing, a good and convincing story about a jazz musician. Callard's musician (a white *British* pianist, what's more) was so credible he put me in mind of several such neglected talents I know. The story is also unromanticized, funny, touching, shrewd about race relations and should be absorbing even to those uninterested in jazz. Callard, who has published biographies of those unusual authors Evelyn Scott and Anna Kavan, is himself thoroughly professional and well worth reading.

All the above stories begin and end especially well; they all have important things to say, and a fine urgency about them. As Carver wrote: 'I like it when there is some feeling of threat or sense of menace in short stories. I think a little menace is fine to have in a short story . . . There has to be tension, a sense that something is imminent, that certain things are in relentless motion, or else, most often, there simply won't be a story.' There was more than a little menace in quite a few of the runners-up. Their material might range from the gothic and gruesome to the deceptively everyday, but they all had that edge, their style well adjusted to or growing from their content. Nothing to choose between them: all are polished, page-turning, exciting in their different ways. Several dealt with violent death, murder and suicide, but all of these extremer or more obviously 'dramatic' stories were handled with considerable style and imagination: the reader might shudder, but fear or sympathy or sadness were aroused, and the narrative impetus never slackened.

Suicide features in a story from New Zealand, David Brown's OFF, a compassionate and haunting character study of a lonely homosexual. Once again, sentimentality is avoided, hence real emotion is aroused. By contrast John Wakeman's THE DEATH OF THE AUTHOR is a hilarious satire on writing workshops, literary critical theorists and gnawing ambition. Wakeman's other submitted story was as good, in its way, but this was funnier – and it's

exceedingly hard to make people laugh. Another talented writer
. . .

CHANGE AT CREWE by William Campbell is one of the most concise and chilling examples of the 'slasher' genre I've read. Thoroughly macabre and unpleasant, but completely and horribly convincing, it moves like an express train right up to the final twist. Unputdownable. (Or should that be 'uncutdownable'?) Also exploring (if in more complex and reflective fashion) the psychology of a killer is the excellent ON THE EDGE by Kevin Parry. Parry's five stories, all with South African settings, were all impressive ones: he's a real writer, with narrative ability and a powerful sense of indignation. This particular exploration of the Boer mind says a lot about racism and hypocrisy, and says it unforgettably. Blanaid McKinney also submitted several stories: these too had their own distinctive voice, but I liked THE GOLD OF TOLOSA best. Here was an unusual view of London, and a compassionate, gentler view of death and dissolution, of memory and love. Another genuine writer, from whom I'm sure more will be heard.

The remaining four runners-up were equally impressive, and they tackled complex and tricky themes – the deaths of relationships, of childhood and innocence – in their difference yet very affirmative ways. LIVESAVING by J.L. Brooke was one of the sparest stories I've read in a long time. Less than five pages suggest a whole saga of marital and family ties turned sour. This description of a small boy's all too brief weekend reunion with his father magically conjures up a whole world of pain and longing in the fewest possible words. THE TIME MACHINE by David Almond is another story dealing with childhood, and whose effect, again through style, is lyrical, poignant and, yes, magical, without sentimentality or cheapness. Two more stories – about separation and failures in intimate relationships – came from Alex Barr, with THE FAN, and, further afield, from Ron Smith in British Columbia – THE LAST TIME WE TALKED. Both stories pleased and moved me; they were precisely and honestly written, and they round off a selection of very talented and convincing runners-up.

Also commended: John Gohorry's IN THE STEINGEBIET; KEEN DISCRIMINATING SIGHT, by H. Cassall, and HAIRPIN BEND by Robert

Dodds. These too were good stories, unlucky not to be among the main prizewinners. It is a pity space does not allow their inclusion in the authology. In the end I felt that this year's winners were even stronger than the 1989 vintage, which still lingers in my memory. It's been a pleasure reading them.

SELIMA HILL

Poetry Report

How do I win? I am often asked this question. *How do I win a Poetry Competition?*
I could answer: write a poem that is alive. That takes you by the hand. That takes risks. That takes off. That shows you care. That's written as if you mean it. This is all very well, you will say, but how do we know if a poem's alive? Or not?

So, rather than vague and evasive answers such as these, I will try and be more practical in my comments.

First of all, *presentation*. And, after five or ten thousand poems, you too, would begin to think it was most important. No coffee-stains, old staples, signs of last-minute splodgy Tippexing-out. No old dates or crossed-out names. On the other hand, elaborate bindings and folders can look a bit silly too. Make space for the poem simply to speak for itself. Above all, get it all on one page if at all possible. I couldn't believe how many poems had their last few lines just dangling pathetically on another sheet.

Subject matter. Remember your poem is one of thousands. It's got to do what it can to *stay on top*. Writing on a well-worn theme will only mean more competition. Probably seven out of ten poems dealt with relationships between partners. Another one or two were about the environment. The popular subjects, then, in more detail were: loneliness, loss, memory, friendship, love, regret; the seasons, pollution, health and health care and recycling. More specific subjects that recurred were: Lockerbie, James Bulger, VE Day, whales and Golden Cap. Other subjects, popular in the media, nevertheless did not appear: football and fashion, for instance. Food. Music. Sport.

Another point. It might be worth familiarising yourself with the judge's work if you are feeling very keen. In my case, for instance, poems about, say, babies or camels or Mongolia were bound to make me feel more involved. And that it is what a poem should aim to do. *Involve the reader* in its life and world.

Poetry Report

Titles. If the typing is like the front garden, the title is like the door. Imagine reading maybe fifty poems called *Spring.* Then meeting one called *How Are We Today* or *I Have Wrapped The Ancestral Ticking Clock* or *So Here It Is Your Stupid Sonnet.* Or how about *Coleridge Goes Scuba Diving, God for Breakfast, The Old Man In My Beer?* They ask you to sit up, don't they? They make you feel you've got company.

Form. I am asked most of all about form. Yes, use form if you can get it absolutely perfect. If you can use the form to say more than you could have without it. I do feel I have a responsibility towards poetry and its practitioners, and I believe skill and tradition should be given all the support they can get. I would always favour, let us say, a sonnet over an otherwise equally strong free-verse poem. I appreciate the *care* of the writer.

Talking of form, a poem turned up which was called a sonnet, but did not look like one. Four concurrent lines were only half-lines: there was a hole on one corner. On reading it, however, I saw that it was about silence, and the poet was well aware of what he or she was doing. Although, in the event, I felt the poem did not add up to more than a comment on form, here was a good example of the need to read each poem right through carefully, and not to dismiss it on sight!

Another formal poem, a villanelle. Again, it didn't look right. There was an extra word in the repeat line. Then I remembered, luckily for our poet, W.H. Auden's villanelle *If I Could Tell You,* which begins 'Time will say nothing but I told you so' and ends:

> 'Will Time say nothing but I told you so?
> If I could tell you I would let you know.'

So, although I did regret the alteration of the repeat, I felt it was not fair to disallow it.

Prizes. This poem, SONGS OF PRAISE, one of several about Lockerbie, wins one of the eight Commendations, for using the villanelle form with such haunting appropriateness. And I hope you enjoy as much as I did the four other quiet Commended poems – the scrupulous THE DYING ROOM, the quirky SANDMAN, the celebratory ROOTS and the clear and dignified EARTH-STARS, the latter a special favourite for attempting a scientific subject and introducing scientific language into 'poetical' space. And I also enjoyed the three noisier ones – the witty and expansive COWS, the energetic FRANK'S OLD MANSION, and the daring CASUALTY. The last line makes me feel *Phew!* I love it!

The *Quartos* prizes, in no particular order, got to three simple but insistent poems I found I kept coming back to, all the more moving for their spareness and sincerity: I LIED, DAD, NIGHT THOUGHTS and THE WHITE SWANS, which reads like a beautiful ballad.

The six supplementary prizewinners, again in no particular order, are: GONE FISHING, a natty and intimate poem with a refreshingly 'go-for-it' ending: 'Her dress finished,/she slips it on/and rows out to catch her man.' I also chose the supple, quietly confident, warm and seductive THE CALL-IN, the bold and intriguing UNDER THE BLUE-PRINTED SKY and the surreal yet tenacious TWO DREAMINGS – feasts for the senses, whose *detail*, as the art historian Robert Hughes has put it, *contradicts sentiment* – sentiment being the trap every poet must learn to avoid. Or, to put it Yeats' way: *All that is personal soon rots. It must be packed in ice.* STRIPWASH is such a poem – icy, chastening, dead steady. It pins you down with its courage and authenticity. OPEN MOUTH, the last of the six runners-up, is in a way the most interesting poem of all. It has certainly caused me the most anxiety! What does it mean? I know it reads well. I know it's up and running. I know it has rewarded my reading and my re-reading. But – to confirm, no doubt, some people's worst suspicions – I have to say I don't know what it's 'about'. Any more than, say, an abstract painting, which nevertheless can have its own meaning, its own convincing and beguiling integrity. Let me quote the final stanza, and see what you think about it:

> With our skin as tight
> as a bird's
> we stood before her.
> She made the noise
> of a quiet birthing animal.
> We looked into her mouth
> and it was full of light.

Poetry Report

Finally, the three main prize-winners, whose bright, fresh, confident living language makes me *hear myself being spoken to*. This is the decisive factor. They kept coming back, like old friends. THE FIRST TOURIST exudes professionalism and inventiveness. It makes you feel at home with the writer. Relaxed. Interested. A pleasure!

The second prize goes to SUN-PATCH – a poem which addresses a difficult subject, perhaps the most 'poetic' of them all – light – and makes not a single mistake. Seamlessness, virtuosity, delightful rhyming. Listen:

> the light/Appears to shake, to flap its golden wings
> As if to flee into the blue. Just seems:
> The patch still sails beyond the shadow, sings
> Still beyond our human being and our dreams.

It makes me think of Robert Frost's delightful description of a poem: 'A poem begins as a lump in the throat, a homesickness; it finds the thought and the thought finds the words.' Thank you.

SCHOOL RULES, unflinching yet stately, was in the end my favourite – a beautifully controlled poem of four short but spacious stanzas. Some of you may feel the subject inappropriate. I trust it is redeemed by the fine feeling and by the infinitely generous last line.

In conclusion, I would like to thank Peggy Chapman-Andrews for her dedication to this inspiring project and, of course, the poets, in whose stimulating company I have spent the last two months, sharing their pain and triumphs, their hopes and fears. I feel I have made many new friends and acquaintances, who obviously enjoy the art of writing as much as I do. As the first prize-winner says, it gives our hearts and souls *a pair of hands*.

RICHARD GRIFFITHS

Watching Men on the Moon

I knelt down beside him so that our faces were level. My condensing breath clouded the space between us. I pointed at the moon and Peter's eyes followed my finger.

'Can you see the face?' I asked.

He looked at me.

'That's the man in the moon,' I said.

I smiled but he did not – his face became very still. His eyes switched back and forth between mine, cross-checking.

He looked up at the sky again: a stiff-limbed cartoon figure in the thick wool of his first coat.

The moon's birthmarked face looked down. Peter seemed not to blink. His wide eyes let the light in raw and unfiltered: he was learning something, fixing it in his mind. I felt a stab of panic: anything might rush in, unchecked. I wanted to take it back, say it's not a real man, but already he was turning his face back to mine.

'There's no-one there,' he said.

He came down to breakfast with that look about him: he'd been reading. I raised the newspaper an inch to hide my eyes. A question was coming.

'Dad.'

That word: an unmanned probe searching for intelligent life. I heard him open the cereal packet.

I folded the paper onto the table and watched him.

'I don't understand what a red shift is,' he said.

Sunday morning.

Aldrin's crew-cut head stared up at me from the front page of the paper and Peter's eyes dropped for a moment from my face to his.

Red shift. I wanted to say *It's what your mother won't wear for me anymore*, but when he looked up at me I shrugged and said, 'I don't know either.'

Watching Men on the Moon

I could hear Janine in the kitchen, the slide of the metal grill pan. I could smell toast.

'Can I see the paper?' He took it before I could answer.

'There's no-one up there,' I said, 'It's all being filmed on a set in Hollywood.'

'Yes but what about the rockets?' He spoke without lifting his head from the paper.

'Just models. Like Sting-Ray.'

'What about the photos then?'

I'd seen them, pictures of the earth half-buried in space, the moon close-to.

'Photographs of paintings.'

Janine came in and she put a plate of toast on the table.

Peter said 'But how would they know it looks like that if they haven't really been there?'

'Who can say it doesn't look like that?' I grinned, 'No-one's been up there to find out.'

Janine glanced at me as she sat down.

'It's true,' I said, 'the Sea of Tranquillity will be the same tonight as it's always been – empty.'

When Peter had finished I got the paper back, and as I read, I could hear the small sounds of Janine's eating.

'You should take him more seriously,' she said, 'There's no need to be so cynical.'

I lowered the paper.

'I do take him seriously. He knows I'm joking. Anyway, I don't want him to believe everything he's told without question.'

Janine examined the surface of her toast carefully.

'That's good,' she said, 'because I believed you without question, once.'

In the hot vacuum of the afternoon, I ran out of things to do. I had read the paper. Peter was out somewhere, Janine was out somewhere else. And I was waiting for them both to return.

I checked my watch. Janine was due back and she had told Peter to be back before her. It would be easier if he was, and I found myself checking my watch again, willing him home.

I picked up the paper and stood by the window with it, searching for something to read, something I had overlooked. Aldrin was missing, cut from the front page. The centre pages, the colour ones, were gone too. Peter cut and collected this stuff every day and he relayed selected details to me in regular teatime transmissions. He knew the flight details by heart: the repeated shedding of used hardware: the three men retreating eventually into the only remaining part. He told me – and I imagined this conversation replayed over thousands of tea-tables each evening – that he wanted to be Neil Armstrong when he grew up. Possibly Buzz Aldrin. Definitely not the third man, who would circle the moon alone whilst the other two walked on the surface.

I checked my watch again and then went upstairs.

In Peter's room his scrapbook of newspaper cuttings lay open on the small table he used as a desk. His telescope stood on the table also, its lenses capped. I sat down and looked at the scrapbook.

I found Aldrin, gummed into place already. I turned back a few pages: stubbled and grimed astronauts grinned from the deck of an aircraft carrier, rows of clean sailors saluted. Back another page: three confident smiles above the metal neck-rings of new white suits.

I flicked further back. *Astronauts die in launch pad fire*: pure breathing-oxygen helping a spark turn into a quick fire, the melting suit-nylon glueing the bodies where they lay. Cries on the radio before the radio burned too. I turned some more pages. It was a language of burns, all of it. Short burns, long burns, timed burns. Silent hauls to imaginary waypoints, waiting for the next burn to keep things on track. I shut the book.

On the wall above Peter's empty pillow, above the curve of the headboard, the earth rose above the lunar horizon.

He had shown me the moon once, let me look through the telescope at the remote and silent disc. I remembered taking my eye from the eyepiece for a few minutes and staring up into the sky with him. When I looked back, the moon's full circle was cut by the dark edge of the telescope lens – something had moved.

'The telescope's slipped,' I had said, holding the tripod and easing the metal tube a fraction to centre the moon again.

I remembered his laugh, 'It's not the telescope moving, Dad, its the earth.'

The tube was warm to my fingers under the late sun as I uncapped the lenses. I could see nothing except the magnified blue of the afternoon. As if the telescope were blind in daylight, whilst at night, with just the least grip of rubber on the formica table and a thumb-tightened wing-nut holding its angle, it would reveal motion that our naked eyes could not detect.

The back door banged and I knew it was Janine. I covered the lenses and left the room, closing the door quietly. I went downstairs.

Janine was in the kitchen. When she saw me she said 'Where's Peter?'

'Not back yet.'

'But it's almost six!' she said, 'I told him to be back by five. Where is he?'

And we were arguing again, until Peter did arrive and his cut lip and bruised face stopped us.

Later, the three of us watched them descend to the moon. Janine's attention flickered between the breathless commentary, Peter's bruises, and a third world of her own.

Peter said, 'Imagine if they can't get back. If they get stuck there.'

'That's why they don't choose young men to go,' I said.

Peter glanced at me, 'Why don't they?'

'Because those men,' I nodded at the television, 'are old enough not to panic if things go wrong. They'd stay calm.'

He was watching the screen again, but thinking about this.

'Look at them,' I said, 'How old are they? In their forties . . .'

'Thirty-nine,' said Peter.

'. . . and all married, with kids, responsibilities. Mature men – psychologically stable.'

Peter frowned and nodded.

Janine was looking at me. Her face was expressionless: whether she saw me or not was impossible to say. I turned back to the television and we watched in silence.

In the end they were down. Their crushed-foil voices spanned the gap back to the earth, where already timers unwound and men made plans for them to leave. The third man orbited.

Peter said, 'They're going to rest now. Before they walk on the moon.'

'And when is that?' Janine said suddenly.

'A bit later,' Peter said, 'After they've rested.'

'Yes, but what time?'

'Later. An hour or something.'

Janine picked up the paper, and turned the pages, one at a time. After a moment she said,

'Four o'clock in the morning, it says here.'

Peter said nothing.

'It's far too late Peter,' she said.

'Yes, but . . .'

He turned to her, and then to me.

'Dad . . .?'

Both of them looked at me.

'You've got school tomorrow,' I said, 'You can't stay up till four o'clock.'

'Well, can I get up then, just for that bit.'

Yes, I wanted to say, *I'll wake you up*. I wanted to see it too. See Armstrong leave the security of their small ship – that little origami ball, all reverse-folds – and climb down the ladder. I wanted to see his hands let go. Listen to his over-sibilant breath wheeze through our cardboard tv-speaker. See whether the cynics would be right and his life support system would pull him over onto his back.

I shook my head.

'But it's the first man on the moon, Dad,' Peter said.

'They'll show it again tomorrow.'

'But that won't be live.'

'Well . . . its not live anyway,' I grinned at him, 'It's a quarter of a million miles from here and the tv signals take . . .'

Janine's eyes narrowed.

'Please, Dad,' Peter said.

'No, Peter,' Janine and I said, together.

We listened to the stamp of his feet on the stairs. After a minute I heard water running in the pipes.

'He can watch it tomorrow,' Janine said, 'Can't he?'

'He can watch it tomorrow.'

She looked at the television for a moment, and then went over and turned it off. The space-talk stopped and she sat down on the settee next to me.

We stared at the empty screen, at our figures in a curved grey living room. Our shoulders touched. The television tube crackled its last static into the dry air and I picked out Janine's bare, pale arms in the glass. The soft spot in the centre of the screen hardened into a tiny star. I wanted to put my arm around her but I did not dare to. The pressure between our shoulders rose and fell as we breathed.

'Will you ask him?' she said, 'Tomorrow?'

She had bathed the bruise on his face and made his lip sting with diluted Dettol, but had got little from him: *just some boys.*

'I'll ask him,' I said.

She put her hand in mine and leaned her head on my shoulder. I could smell her hair. She felt like someone new, and it seemed possible, then, to fix everything.

So I said, 'I'm sorry, Janine.'

For a moment the word hung in the room with nowhere to go and I wondered whether she had understood. But then she moved, slowly and carefully. *Sorry* – that small explosive charge of a word. She detached her hand from mine, lifted her head from my shoulder, and drew back along the settee until she was separate and still.

'I waited for you,' she said calmly, 'I waited whilst the two of you made up your minds. I could put up with being chosen, but not with waiting and I had to wait a long time.'

Her eyes were fixed points. I wanted mine to be too, but they circled, skirting the edges of her face, sightlessly tracing the hem of her dress.

'I told myself I shouldn't wait, that I should take Peter and go.'

She smoothed her dress against her legs and cupped her knees in her hands.

'I couldn't understand what was going through your mind,' she said, 'I thought, either you wanted me, or you didn't.'

She stood up.

'I'm going to bed now. It makes me tired thinking about it. I know you're sorry.'

After she had gone I sat for a while on my own. I imagined them on the moon, somewhere above my head, resting. Waiting to put on their helmets and let the air escape into the vacuum so they could open the door.

The next evening we watched them walking on the moon, bowl-faced in the harsh sunlight. We listened to their radioed conversations. But Peter was right, it wasn't the same because we knew all along what was going to happen.

Janine kept trying to catch my eye. I had not asked Peter, he seemed okay. School fights were things that happened to everyone eventually.

'If their radios broke,' Peter said, without turning from the television, 'Do you know what they would do?'

I did not.

They'd touch visors,' he said, 'Because then they could talk to each other, even without radios, because their voices would go through the helmets enough for them to hear each other.'

'You mean sort of like tin-cans on strings?' I asked.

'No, he doesn't,' Janine said, to make me look at her. I did and she mouthed *ask him.*

He was reading a book by the light from his bedside lamp when I opened the door to his room. I closed the door behind me and knelt next to the bed.

'What are you reading about?' I could see it was an astronomy text book.

'The Doppler Effect,' he said, 'I still don't understand what a red shift is.'

I looked at the upside-down diagrams.

'It says it's like trains and fire-engines going past,' he said.

'You know as much as I do,' I said, 'More.'

After a moment he asked 'What's the matter?'
'Nothing,' I answered, 'I just wanted to see how your face is.'
His eyes dropped to the book, 'It's okay.'
The light gleamed on his hair.
'Do you want to tell me?'
'What?'
'Who it was.'
'Just some boys,' he said, and turned the page. The sound of his fingers against the paper cut gently across his voice. 'It doesn't matter.'
'Well . . . tell me if it happens again.'
'It won't.'
He turned another page, too soon to have read it.
I lifted my knees from the floor and crouched on my toes. The walls had changed since I had last been in the room – the earth had moved. It now rose above the moon on the wardrobe door and above the bed, Aldrin stood on lunar dust potato-printed with deep boot-marks.
Peter spoke. 'I want to leave school. Get a job, like you.'
He was still pretending to read.
'Don't wish your life away,' I said, 'When you get a job, you'll wish you were at school again.'
'Why?' He looked up from his book and the bedside lamp was a twin spark on his eyes.
I tried to think of something as we stared at each other, but then he looked back at his book, embarrassed.
The blood prickled slowly back into my legs as I stood up and went to the door. At the door I turned. The near side of Peter's face was in shadow, the light from the lamp spilled across the wall behind him.
'Five more minutes, okay?'
'Okay.' He did not look up.
I looked at Aldrin again, at the smooth convexity of his visor. It was impossible to guess what he was thinking, whether he was glad to be there or desperately wanted to come back: his face only showed the moon's dry soil. The horizon in his visor matched the real one behind him so that his helmet seemed empty. He was

round shouldered and fat-limbed in his suit, the thick material made his right arm stick out from his body even though it hung relaxed at his side. He stood awkwardly, mid-gesture, padded legs uncomfortably far apart. His knees were dirty.

I slipped from the room and closed the door on him: a kid in a coat.

They had left the moon, and there were rumours already that the trip had not been everything it seemed. I had heard that Armstrong had dithered before committing himself to a landing, held off from the surface, not liking what he saw, reaching into the last few seconds of his fuel. I thought of what they had left behind: a limp, coat-hangered flag; footprints trapped like fossils under the windless sky.

And then I went back downstairs to talk to Janine.

PETER REGENT

The Blessed Hieronymus

Deserts often seem curiously insubstantial. It is as if they stunned the senses with their immensity and their stupendous heat. The sun rules: its terrible brightness beats back from glassy drifts of sand, reverberates from crazed mudflats and bounces off bleached rocks. Stones that would be bruisingly solid if you fell on them must be squinted at through one eye, so that volume and substance become uncertain. Far things corruscate; the horizon quivers, liquid and ambiguous. But for all their evanescent appearances, deserts are harsh places, and often fatal – that is why they are deserted.

But all things are relative. Very few deserts are entirely void of human life. Thus, in the early years of Christianity, the wilderness of the Thebaid contained a sparse scattering of nomadic tribes, innocent of agriculture and clothing, and an even smaller population of religious hermits, troglodytic or stylitic according to their preference for the indoor life of a cave or the airiness of a column.

The hermit Hieronymus, already a saint in the opinion of devout ladies in the nearest settlements, was one among that holy dispersion – it can hardly be called a company – of solitaries. He was, when this narrative opens, sitting outside his cave, contemplating the evening and awaiting a party of female enthusiasts. The low angle of the sun threw into relief what had been beaten flat by the vertical rays of noon, and the reduced intensity of light permitted colour – reds, ochres, and blue shadows – to reinvest the landscape.

At an immense height above the saint's pate, vultures soared. Their hunched heads, as bald as his, turned this way and that in their grim inquisition of the desert floor. The saint watched their circling. He pondered their spiritual significance, contrasting them with the white gulls that he had once seen far to the North. They, too, pared the air, sharp-eyed for filth – only Hieronymus did not know their habits, and found in them a symbol of the immaculate soul wandering in an unredeemed world, longing for union with the infinite. Vultures, on the other hand – such consummate aviators must have been set in the sky as symbols of angelic aspiration, dragged down by lust to foulness and ordure.

The saint's pious reflections ran away with him. At the thought of carrion his mind was invaded by images of bazaar women, dancing with bellies rippling like sackfuls of rodents. He felt himself falling like a stooping vulture, from the upper strata of asceticism to the reeking mortality of the cadaver – inevitably, a female cadaver. He shook his head, laughing at his own foolishness, and reaching for his scourge.

The life of a desert anchorite is hard, but Hieronymus was perennially cheerful; that was part of his sanctity. He accepted everything, if not with equanimity, with glee – chuckling as he scolded the bees that stung him as he reached for a portion of their honey, giggling when the dried carob husks on which he lunched cracked another tooth, smiling sweetly when the gentle ladies that came to see him shuddered at his supper of yellow grubs and ants. He would playfully scold the ladies for their niceness, then turn to the serious matter of instructing the younger ones in the preservation of virginity. And after they and their sunshade-bearing negroes had gone, he would whip himself – not for having contemplated fair skins and delicately-formed lips, for he had steeled himself against such things long ago – but for having accepted the homage of their admiring eyes.

Occasionally, the saint was visited by a detachment of cavalry from the garrison that maintained a Roman presence along the desert's edge. The troops remained at a respectful distance, while the captain dismounted and came to sit stiffly by the austere figure in the cave-mouth and maintain a few minutes' clipped conversation – for the hermits were a useful source of intelligence about the movements of the local tribes. The army longed to send the nomads packing, across the desert to where the Abyssinians ate people raw. Hieronymus was sweetly deprecatory, but the officer gathered that he, too, detested the heathens, with their thoughtless abandonment to the hunt for food, their sensuous enjoyment of the sun, of pools of clear water, of children and bright adornments.

The Blessed Hieronymus

Above all, he deplored the shamelessness of their women, brazen in their bangled nudity.

At first the nomads had been ashamed of their nakedness. The tall, thin girls had been coy before the saint's stern gaze. But that was at first. Now they were at best indifferent, practising their filthy habit of washing from head to toe in the pool that was fed by the spring from which he drank, and flaunting their streaming bodies as they did so. Sometimes they teased him; breaking into spasms of dance before his very eyes – their funny, sidling back-and-forth dance, with all their limbs open to the concupiscent admiration of their unfortunate menfolk. They laughed when the saint scolded them. They ran away, and threw pebbles at him.

The expected visitors arrived. Hieronymus declined the gifts they brought, and they barely nibbled at the dish of chopped pods and thistles that he offered. He answered their questions with endearing modesty, his childish innocence shining in his face. When a matron, too patrician to be shushed by her companions, ventured to ask why he chose to live in the desert at such an inconvenient distance from town, Hieronymus smiled, and explained that he was a weak, silly fellow, so he had come into the wilderness to avoid distraction.

'Distraction?'

The saint giggled in his holy innocence.

'You mean, to escape temptation?' The matron gathered her sweet, ogling daughters into the protection of her splendid arms.

'And to avoid the occasion of sin,' the saint added, shyly.

The matron lowered her gaze and wearily considered her splendid hips. Hieronymus meanwhile reflected on the beauties of continence, and reminded himself of sweat and cesspits, and how such things were inseparable from human company. He spoke of his need for peace, in which to contemplate.

'Ah, yes. Contemplation. But what have you been contemplating all this time? What is there to think about –' the speaker waved a magnificent arm at the surrounding desolation '– here?'

Hieronymus sighed. 'God.'

'God?'

'– and what keeps us from him.'
'And what is that?'
'Sin.'

The matron thought of reckless daughters and impecunious suitors. The plumper of the two girls thought of sweetmeats, and long dresses in the oriental silks that were just coming in, but her younger sister leaned forward eagerly:

'Tell us what we must do!'

The saint's emaciated body quivered with enthusiasm as he addressed her fresh and dimpled beauty: 'Guard your treasure intact! It is your gift for God.' His eyes rolled up in ecstasy as he mentally contemplated the smooth, round integrity of bodies incapable of sin. In the voice of prophesy he cried: 'Let no man seek to re-enter the gate by which he fell into the World! It leads to the nothingness whence he came, instead of eternal life. Oh, blessed virginity!'

The saint fell back, exhausted. 'Yes, well . . .' said the matron. She led her little party in a gathering-up of skirts, and the attendant negroes bowed it into litters. With fluttering fans and swaying sunshades the entourage wound away through the drifts and spreading shadows of the desert evening.

When the visitors had gone, darker figures emerged to whisper round the cave-mouth. Sharp elbows nudged skinny ribs at the sound of a leather thong striking flesh. The tribespeople hid when the saint limped out to press his excoriated back on the salty encrustation of a rock. He moaned, then rubbed himself on the harsh surface, to punish his self-pity. A smothered giggle came from behind a clump of thorns, and Hieronymus scolded like an angry squirrel. Two naked figures broke cover and ran away. One of them was female, and in his pain the saint roared:

'Filthy imp of Satan – whore!'

The plumper of the two backsides wagged coquettishly, and Hieronymus reached for his whip again. As the lash bit into his raw back, he was racked by an even more exquisite torment – didn't perverse sensuality tread on thorns and swoon with pleasure? Might there be sin in the very act of self-mortification? He redoubled his frenzied lashing, conscious that the creatures were laughing at him, and that one of the girls was slim and pretty. Lash! lash! lash! – oh, it was a hard life, to be a saint!

To strengthen himself against temptation, Hieronymus wrapped a threadbare blanket into a bundle, and set off on a journey deeper into the desert. On the first day he was beset by images of noble women walking at his side in diaphanous draperies, smiling at him. Sometimes they skipped ahead to dance the nomads' sidling dance, veils flying, or cast aside entirely. On the second day, beasts coupled all round him. Mice conducted their shrill amours at his feet; insects mated as they buzzed round his head; stallions reared up in their pride, hoofs flying and teeth bared as they mounted round-rumped mares; lions and leopards roared, and slaked their turbulent lusts so close that he choked on their blood-reeking breath. On the third day, on all sides of his path there was fornication between men and women, women and women, men and men, devils and women, men and angels . . . Hieronymus drew his whip from his bundle and lashed his tormentors. Their only response was to multiply their perversions, screaming with laughter. He turned back.

About a day's march from his cave, he reached a place where water bubbled up from under some rocks. A little stream flowed away with a lovely, low sound, till it was lost in a patch of thin grass to which the nomads often brought their goats. Hieronymus drank and gave thanks at the spring. As he rested, he became aware of a scuffling and grunting noise, coming from behind the next outcrop. Now that the phantoms had left him, he thought it might be a wild beast – real, this time. Probably it was only goats, but even so he must beware, for he-goats leapt she-goats with no consideration for ascetic eyes. One dreadful day he had surprised two shepherd children in the very act, but this hoarse sound promised some still more awful sight that might mortify the eyes to the soul's advantage. Cautiously, he looked over the crest of the rocks. At first he thought the strange, grey creature on the other side was four-legged; then he saw that it was a human being, bent double, and intent on some obscure snuffling activity. Hieronymus gripped his whip – surely there would be work for it here! – and peered harder. Was the creature praying to a stone, perhaps? He shaded his eyes and glared. It was not. It was eating grass.

An aged human being was grazing like a beast – naked! The saint's first impulse was one of indignation, then he realized that a being capable of such self-mortification must be very holy – unless, of course, he was a follower of the execrable Arius, or a devotee of Neo-Platonism, Manichaeism, or Gnosticism. The proper course was to propose a disputation, with a view to mutual illumination and the expulsion of error. Hieronymus called out to the herbivore.

The creature raised its head. It was as if a lump of rock and weed were taken by surprise. Straggling grey locks fell about a face where more wisps of hair were confused with the shreds of grass that hung from an astonished mouth. The saint called again, and the creature sprang up, leaping over the rocks with surprising agility, and fled across the burning plain.

'Wait for me, for God's sake,' cried the saint, as he gave chase.

The reply came in a voice at once shrill and hoarse, like that of the mad bird that utters its cracked-bell cry among the rocks: 'Leave me alone, for God's sake!'

Hieronymus was hindered by his bundle, so he threw it away, but still the naked figure scampered on in front. The saint's ragged garments encumbered him, so he flung them off as he ran, but still the withered buttocks twinkled ahead, until the ancient runner had completed a circle and come back to the rocks from which the chase had started. Now the fugitive clambered over the stones like a goat. At the summit of the rocks he turned his head, and gasped: 'Because you threw away the things of this world – even your clothes – I will speak to you, thought I cannot bear the smell of men.'

'Tell me', panted Hieronymus, 'How can you live as you do, eating grass, and going naked without sin.'

'Avoid all men, and never speak!' said the other, and leapt down out of sight on the other side of the rocks.

Hieronymus climbed after him. 'I, too, cannot bear the company of men,' he puffed.

'Then stop following me,' came the reply.

'But I wish to dispute with you,' and Hieronymus clambered among the rocks between which the other had disappeared.

He searched for a long time, till a wild goat sprang up at his feet and clattered away over the stones. He followed, and it led him into a cave. The grass-eater was crouched inside, facing him for the first time and evidently taken by surprise. The saint's astonishment was as great, for despite the clutching gesture of modesty, it was clear that he was in the presence of a woman. He reeled in horror.

'Hag!' he hissed. 'Jezebel!' and he advanced, cracking his whip.

'I begged you not to follow me,' said the anchoress.

'Source of all evil – cause of Man's downfall!' cried Hieronymus.

'Eve brought only knowledge of the evil that already existed.'

'Fountain of God's displeasure!'

'If God was displeased, he knew evil for the first time, and by virtue of Eve's indiscretion, he was made truly omniscient.'

'Impious, blaspheming hag!' roared Hieronymus. He felt a new kind of fury, different from his chaste indignation with the heathen, at the spectacle of this dreadful female anatomy exhibiting rationality and pretending to holiness. He leapt at the hag. She tried to escape, but her sinewy limbs were powerless against the accumulated tension of forty years' suppressed libido. The hag howled; Hieronymus roared, and at the mouth of the cave naked savages gathered, wide-eyed at the spectacle of the saint making furious jig-a-jig with the holy woman.

Awe-struck, they crept away, and were waiting when Hieronymus staggered out into the air. 'Apes! Inverted souls! Shameless filth! Barbarians! Catamites! Huzzies!' he hissed to their shocked, uncomprehending faces. When he had limped his blood-encrusted flanks away, they crept into the cave and covered the old woman's battered corpse with husks and dried leaves from the tree that grew beside her secret spring.

A few days later, the Captain came to where Hieronymus sat in his cave-mouth. He tapped his cane against his boot and talked, in his clipped and businesslike way. He asked if the saint had seen anything of the Holy Agrippina '– a lady in your line of country,

Padre. A bit short in the shift, from what I hear – a bit short in the marbles too, if you ask me – but undoubtedly a very holy lady. Did you know her?'

'I flee from the smell of men – that includes women,' replied Hieronymus.

'Pity you two never met.'

'I have not heard the name. Is she well with God?'

'A couple of my chaps found her – raped, mutilated and murdered.'

'God be praised that she has found bliss at last.'

'It's those savages, of course. They'd tried to hide the body under dried leaves – quite stupid. They're just animals, really,' and the captain described the state of the corpse.

'Tsk tsk!'

'You can say that again, Padre.'

'You are sure they did it?' The saint's mild eye looked sideways at the captain.

'Well, I didn't do it, and there isn't anyone else for miles around – except you, and I don't suppose you did it, Padre.'

Hieronymus giggled in his holy innocence.

'Murdering black bastards!' said the captain. 'Now, you're a thinking sort of chap, Padre. What do you make of it?'

'We each share in our brother's sin,' said Hieronymus.

'Mystic shit, Father. They did it, and I'll see they jolly well pay. We simply can't allow this sort of thing. It's an insult to the state, a threat to public order and an affront to decency and morals. Now's the time to deal with it once and for all. It might be you next!'

Hieronymus made a depreciatory gesture, but the Captain persisted: 'It's time for a final solution.'

'If it brought repentance it would be a mercy.'

'I'll show them what I mean by mercy,' said the Captain. He whacked his boot with his cane, and left.

The saint flogged himself, for gossiping.

When the Captain returned, it was at the head of a long column of naked prisoners, each slender black neck yoked to the next. He gave the order to halt, and strolled across to where Hieronymus sat praying.

'They did it, all right. I had a word with a couple of their leaders – strung 'em up over a campfire. They confessed everything.'

'Suffering may open hearts,' said Hieronymus.

'I couldn't agree more, Padre. Nothing like a bit of the old bonfire, what?'

The saint giggled. 'I must not speak too much with men,' he said.

'Suit yourself, Padre. By the way, I thought I'd carry out sentence here, if you don't mind. Your little stone-pile makes a nice landmark.'

Hieronymus continued his life as an anchorite for many years. Parties of ladies continued to visit him, and to be inspired by his holy innocence, for he exhorted young women to preserve their purity with all the fervour of a modern politician exhorting a nation to preserve its currency from inflation. When he finally died, he had eaten nothing but desert herbs – a dry, prickly, but aromatic diet – for a very long time. His corpse did not putrify. In the dry desert air what little flesh remained on his bones quickly completed the already advanced process of dessication, and retained an agreeable herbal odour that was clear proof of his sanctity. For years his dry and frugal diet had generated only a single adamantine stool each month. A modest cache of these, resembling fossilized truffles and sweetly perfumed, was discovered near his cave after his death. Finely mounted in silver, and installed above altars, they are reported to have worked several miracles.

D.A. CALLARD

Take the 'A' Train

Somewhere in the distance the wind collided with a swing door causing it to flutter and give off a sound which echoed down the vacant corridors like the patter of retreating feet. Hugo was used to that one now, as he was used to the profound submarine crashes which issued without apparent cause form the area of the empty swimming pool. The building was quiet this evening. Only the sound of setting concrete and settling brickwork, amplified by the surrounding vacancy, kept up a constant pinging and popping to disturb his concentration.

For four nights now he had been promised a partner for his vigil but mercifully none had arrived. They would rarely last more than a week, picking up their pay and disappearing on a bender, paying their bills, gambling debts, girlfriend's abortions or whatever: whatever had drawn them from the daytime world to earn a few shillings more keeping nightlong watch over an empty building. In the unlikely event of a break-in, the order was to sound the alarm and run. One person could do this as easily as two, but two was what regulations demanded and two it was, when the other showed up. They invariably fell into one of three categories of obsessive; alcoholic, narcotic or erotic, but Hugo had his own obsession and prayed sometimes for an obsessed rhythm section to augment his own silent solo.

He turned once more to the wooden dummy keyboard on the table and picked idly. He composed in a silence as absolute as Beethoven's, the notes existing only in an amalgam of memory and imagination. It was, he told himself, one of the trials which every artist must endure and, when the specialist jazz record company in Brighton issued his album in the usual limited edition of five hundred, 'two hundred to be distributed by the artist in lieu of royalties', then the sleeve note would record that all composition took place, at night, on a dummy keyboard. 'Brixton Variations' was the current title, 'Brixton Nocturnes' having been ditched as

Take the 'A' Train

being too pretentious. Jazz buffs of the future would come here not to work out or play squash but because here, in the yet-incomplete Brixton Leisure Centre in the summer of 1981, the work which had dragged British jazz out of tired post-Parkerism on the one hand and aleatory honking and screeching on the other had been composed, on a wooden keyboard, by nightwatchman Hugo James.

He felt this way round midnight. The trough did not begin until one in the morning, spiralling down to the four a.m. panic, a jerky stomach and rising aluminium bile. There were the debts, four grand at the last count though he had taken wise advice and stopped counting some months ago. At least mortgage payments were down to three months but only at the cost of pushing credit cards to their limits. There were only five more payments on the electric piano but everything told him that if he didn't get into synthesisers right now the ship of musical history would set sail without him. And there was this friend who roadied for a rock band, some on-hit combo of floppy haired youths who had just split up and had a synth to sell, state of the art, a steal at £800. If it were up to him he would have it, but Terri had put her foot down and, well, yes, maybe now that he was a family man mortgage-strapped for a doll's house in Peckham, hunted by creditors and dependent on his wife's salary for any sort of survival, some might argue that his priorities should lie elsewhere. Terri did. Probably the only reason that they didn't argue more about money was that there wasn't the time, since he got home from work just as she was going out and his evenings were all used up with practices and gigs.

Well, gig, to be more accurate. To be precise, a weekly residence at The Fox and Firkin, Stockwell, with two guys who were emphatically pre-Parker; both college lecturers out for nothing more than a night away from their wives and a chance to impress impressionable girl students with as much idea of jazz as of gamelan. 'The Bud James Three' emitted a mixture of showtime standards, Ellingtonia and MJQ with a fair degree of competence to an indifferent audience of Irish brickies, medallion men looking for local sophistication and any other stray seeking shelter for the evening. They had been gigging there since it reopened after refurbishment with horse-brasses and coaching lamps: the tenor set by M.C. Jimmy who announced, on their opening night, 'Direct from the West End, the fabulous Bud James Three with that classic favourite,' a fumble here for the programme list, 'Take thee a train!'

Hugo had waited for the informed laughter of the crowd, but there was none as the crowd was not informed. In vengeance he sent out the tardy drinkers at closing time with cascades of Cecil Taylor. 'Tune up before you start, not after,' said the last voice through the door. Since then they played 'Take the 'A' Train' as an opener every night, sometimes as finale too: halfway between a theme tune and private joke. Like everything else, the joke turned sour at four in the morning.

The door fluttered once more in the distance causing the illusion of footsteps. Hugo stared at the dumb keyboard. Cecil Taylor had washed dishes for years in New York before being recognised. Mingus in the madhouse. Bird a bloated corpse in the bathroom. Van Gogh's bloody ear. The artist must suffer.

'The artist must suffer.' He liked the phrase. He repeated it aloud savouring its cadence against the bare plaster. He repeated it again and again, accented in French, German, Italian, like an aged Viennese sage, like a Southern Bluesman, like a Venetian Contessa, like a Noel Coward fop: 'The artist must suffer. Ze artiste he must-a sufffferrrrrr, th'artist he gotta suffer, pay his dues, die artist, e musta . . .'

Some modulation of the echo of his ravings indicated a change in the room. Hugo swung around, hunching his shoulders, cringing. Through eyes half-closed with embarrassment he met the impassive gaze of a smartly dressed black man looking down on him with no curiosity or surprise.

'Mr. Costello of the agency sent me. I am the new watchman. You are Mr. James, I believe?'

Hugo stood, flinching, and met his proffered hand. Such was the simple dignity of the introduction that he bowed slightly. As they shook hands the man pressed downward twice with his thumb. A Mason? Hugo thought, before dismissing the idea as ridiculous.

Take the 'A' Train

'My name is Tom Osadebai. You may call me Tom if you like. May I call you Hugo?'

Hugo, still shrivelled with embarrassment, nodded. They sat on opposite sides of the table. 'Please continue with what you were doing,' the man said. Hugo cringed again, wondering whether he expected him to continue his monologue before pretending to recommence his efforts at composition.

'Depth' was probably the best word to describe it, Hugo thought. He and Tom had kept up their vigil for a week now during which time fragments of Tom's history had emerged without cohering into a whole. He had once been headmaster of a school in Nigeria but had come to England to work, successively, as post office casual, street sweeper and nightwatchman. At first Hugo assumed him to be a refugee, a suggestion politely quashed by Tom, who gave the impression of being above politics. When Hugo began his bluffer's guide to African music, Tom quietly closed his eyes and shook his head. 'Mozart was the only musician. Maybe Bach.' He lived in a bedsit somewhere in the wasteland of squats and skips where Brixton faded into the permanent autumn of Camberwell and sent money back to a wife and children at home; unseen for four years now and with no return in the foreseeable future. 'Gravitas' might be a better word especially when, at four or five, the dawn light seeped through the crack in the swing doors and fell on his face in the perfect rest of sleep or meditation, immobile and charged as an Ife bronze.

The fragments of his story were there: his childhood in the mission schools and how he had grown believing that white men were endowed by birth with a virtue denied his feckless countrymen. 'You do not know, Hugo, will never know, the damage that the white man has done to the African psyche.' Tom's impassive face twitched, a slight spasm; he sighed and Hugo felt a surge of pity as if clouds had parted momentarily to reveal some scene of slaughter. Tom's eyes closed, his face rested once more. Hugo was suddenly struck by the pettiness of his own predicament; to be worried by a few paltry debts, some minor musical difficulties.

One night there was a marked change in his demeanour, some

air of barely suppressed joy. He pored intently over papers he kept producing from a document case while Hugo tinkered silently on his keyboard. Some urgency had gone from his composition since Tom had shown a distaste for jazz, and Hugo was coming to feel that there had never been any real profundity, just the disaffected graffiti of a musical adolescent. After an hour or so he slammed down an imaginary lid and looked at Tom.

'Good news?'

Tom raised his eyes and looked at Hugo as if reading an unimaginable sagacity into the simple question. 'Hugo. You are . . . an educated man?'

Hugo shrugged. It was a generous estimate of a BA Humanities Second Class, but probably valid in the world of nightwatchmen.

'Do you have any interest in spiritual philosophy? By this I mean the position of man on earth and his relationship with higher powers?'

Hugo's heart sank. Was the depth and gravitas the outward show of a Plymouth Brethren or Jehovah's Witness?

'I used to meditate, but I couldn't seem to get it to work. I was brought up a Christian. My father was a vicar. I don't practise myself.'

Tom nodded. 'Did you know by the way that the word "vicarious" derives from the word "vicar"?' Hugo shook his head. 'I mean no insult to your father of course,' Tom continued, fingering his papers thoughtfully. 'Do you know what Cabala is?'

Hugo weighed his words carefully. 'It's an ancient system of Jewish mysticism. A way of ordering the world. A way of explaining the meaning of the Scriptures.' Tom nodded, waiting for more. 'A sort of . . . magic?'

'Yes', Tom hissed. 'A sort of magic. Older even than the Jews. I have studied it since I was eighteen. My father before me.'

'In Africa?' Hugo struggled to suppress his incredulity.

'Yes. In Africa. The Dark Continent.' Tom's irony was unexpectedly savage. 'Does it surprise you that Cabala is strong in Africa? I see it does. You think we are all animists, fetishists, practitioners of obeah. When the white man came with Christ he was too weak for our gods. The Masons came but even with Christ they were too weak for our gods. Then we learned Cabala. Cabala with Christ can defeat obeah. From eighteen until I was forty four I studied. I reached the highest grade possible to me. Then my teacher sent me to see the biggest obeah man of the Yoruba. Whole villages work for him. He has fourteen wives. He is so fat he cannot walk without a stick. I went to his hut. He welcomed me. "I saw you coming, little one," he said and projected himself around the hut, blocking all means of escape. I was paralysed. "Now, escape, little one," he said.'

'And?'

Tom threw his head back and laughed for the first time. Scooping his hands upward from the table he threw them toward Hugo's face making him blink involuntarily. 'I threw dust in his eye! I threw dust in his eye! I threw dust in his eye!' the words emerging through cascades of laughter. Hugo tried to open his eyes but they were flecked, rheumy with some of the cement which hung in the air and, blinking, he could just see Tom quaking with suppressed laughter. By the time his vision had cleared, Tom was his old self again, the ghost of a smile playing around his lips.

Three weeks had passed since that night during which Hugo had begged Tom to teach him the rudiments of Cabala. Tom said that he would ask his teachers, but in the meantime he could demonstrate his sincerity by mastering the Hebrew alphabet. The way was difficult, Tom warned. Renunciations, sacrifices and tests would have to be undergone. Tom had had to leave his country, wife, family and a comfortable job to live among strangers, friendless apart from his teachers, to labour among the lowest. Hugo consoled himself that all this was years in his future by which time, at the very least, he would be a living giant of British jazz.

For the grand-daughter of an Amsterdam rabbi, Terri took a dim view of this new enthusiasm. His musical friends were similarly unimpressed. Perhaps he belonged to a credulous generation or perhaps it was just the people he knew, but that part of the jazz avant-garde which was not schismatic Albanian Maoist spent its free time getting stoned and reading The Book of Coming Forth By Day or the Popol Vuh. Cabalism, he gathered, was just a bit too mainstream to be interesting. Nonetheless he let it be known that he was engaged in a long composition entitled 'Toward Ein Soph'; a distant goal really since he still couldn't remember which letter followed Yod and since, thus far, it was merely 'Brixton Variations' retitled.

Events of the prior three weeks would have had a Major Adept tearing his hair. The debt problem had graduated from critical to terminal and there was nothing to be done but to fold one's arms and await the bailiffs. The bassist of the Bud James Three failed to show one night and word came that he had quit his job and marriage for a new life with a girl from Second Year Graphics. Hugo tried to convince the drummer that a piano and drum combo was a daring new jazz format but it didn't wash, and the Bud James Three became the Bud James One. The compositions were unattended, the practices missed: everything narrowed quickly to Cabala, the long nights alone with Tom in the stark deserted room.

Cycling through Brixton the following evening Hugo saw an incident; one of the street Rastas being hustled off by six cops, their truncheons drawn against a threatening mob. It was nothing he hadn't seen before and he didn't even bother to mention it to Tom when he got to work. Looking back over that summer with hindsight, there had been a lot more blue in the street: a lot more blue and a lot more black, fretfully rubbing against one another. He had seen these things but somehow they didn't register.

The previous night The Bud James One played the Fox and Firkin for the first and last time and M.C. Jimmy, paying a third of the fee, mentioned that a video jukebox had been ordered and Hugo's services were no longer needed. In his pocket Hugo carried three letters spewed by unfeeling computers in Northampton, Southend-on-Sea and Bingley. These he added to the pile of unopened demands he kept in his locker at work, away from Terri's eyes. The crunch was coming. Soon. How long, Lord, how long?

Tom was reading when Hugo arrived, absorbed in a fresh communication from the Masters. A week before he had told Hugo that they had given approval to his acceptance as a neophyte which, in turn, allowed him to rise a further grade on the Order. 'Now I am allowed to teach,' he remarked, 'my progress will depend on your progress.' Hugo chilled. What if he turned out a dud, a flunker of CSE Cabala perched endlessly on the bottom branch of the great Tree of Life? Sensing his apprehension, Tom added, 'I know you will not fail me, Hugo.' Another chill. 'But I know I will,' Hugo wanted to say. It even made things better when Tom asked him for £20, 'to defray expenses.' Money somehow squared the situation.

Tom remained preoccupied and Hugo sank into the pleasant torpor which he always felt in his presence. He had heard of this from others who claimed to have found spiritual masters but had never believed it. He had tried to explain it to Terri. In fact, it had been the last time they had spoken. 'Relaxed satisfaction, like after a good meal or mulled wine,' he had said, and she had exploded. Then he tried, 'like an old married couple sitting at the fireside not needing to talk,' and she had stormed out. Probably she was at her mother's. It had happened before.

Tom looked up. 'How are you this evening?'

'Fine,' Hugo lied. 'And you?'

'Fine also. Could you recite the Hebrew alphabet please?'

Hugo recited it faultlessly.

Somewhere in the distance the wind collided with a swing door causing it to flutter and give off a sound which echoed down the vacant corridors like the patter of retreating feet. The wind brought a smell of burning, and voices, jumbled and chaotic. The smell of an African village at nightfall: strange lights flickered through the topmost windows, faint but perceptible. Hugo looked up at Tom. His papers abandoned, he sat crouched yet upright staring as if through the wall to where some ancient enemy, animal or tribal, lurked beyond sight. The jumble of voices grew more distinct and menacing.

'Something is happening, Hugo. We should go and look.'

Hugo nodded. Together they walked through the area of the empty swimming pool, down the corridor whose door always fluttered and out to the great window which looked over the street. Below them, Brixton was ablaze.

Neither spoke. The massed rioters and police moved balletically, the occasional flare of a petrol bomb exploding to illuminate this rank, that formation. Hugo's imagination flashed back to the political hallucinations of his youth when the set-piece confrontations of Grosvenor Square were meant to catch a fire which would never go out. His mouth parched with anticipation and he felt the faint stirrings of an erection. The strangled exhortation, 'Rise! Rise!' which ended one of the Beatles albums ran through his head. He turned to Tom and saw his rapt face charged with fear, his hand rhythmically and automatically crossing and recrossing his heart. 'I did not think it would come so soon,' he heard him murmur.

Hugo snapped into present time. 'We'd better phone Costello and find out what to do,' he suggested.

Tom made the call, but in the silent echoing room, Costello's Belfast koine was audible and urgent. 'The fucking niggers are going apeshit. Put the fucking lights out and get the fuck out of there.'

Tom replaced the receiver without answering. They threw the main switch and crept through the darkness to the obscure side exit which was their usual entry and exit.

'Are you going home?' Hugo asked Tom.

Tom shook his head. He gave Hugo a spare key in case they were separated and together they walked out into the street.

The police had vanished temporarily. Shops were being arbitrarily looted and torched: a few rioters, lacking an outside enemy, fought among themselves. A middle-aged man reeled by carrying a ghetto-blaster attuned to police frequencies. He stopped and stared at a white man with long greasy hair accompanied by a tall black man who might have been a model for police ethnic recruitment. Clearly beyond speech, the man nodded then broke into a smile. He offered the bottle to Tom, who refused it, and to Hugo who did likewise, though he needed a drink. Shrugging, he put the radio down, took a long draught then reeled on, leaving the radio where it stood. Hugo waited for Tom's response, eager to pick it up. Tom did not move. Finally Hugo reached down and Tom shook his head savagely. Rather than leave an uncompleted act, Hugo found a reggae station, turned up the volume and placed it on a wall. A small knot of young looters, temporarily becalmed, looked their way and cheered. Hugo looked at Tom for his reaction. He was smiling in that faintly supercilious headmasterly fashion.

They walked on. Hugo was struck by the carnival atmosphere. A phrase from the old days about revolution being a festival of the oppressed came into his head. A van which had evaded police cordons came down the street and backed up to an electrical goods store where the driver started loading it with televisions, as casually as if he were an employee.

Tom tutted. 'Hugo, what does a man want with more than one television? Must he have a television for his bathroom, his kitchen and his toilet? This man is suffering from Greed. Because it is there he must take. He does not think of the man whose shop it is, or a man who has no television, he thinks only of himself. Ah, Hugo, these people were once my brothers and this is what they have become. Your baubles, your cars and televisions, your white man's toys, your sharp suits, your fat blonde women are ju-ju to them.'

The vision of slaughter glimpsed momentarily between clouds again swamped Hugo. He wanted to tell Tom that if he had a van he would fill it, he would steal the whole of Brixton to be free of debt, to give Terri a good life, to be able to pursue his music. He wanted to say that if the world was corrupt then we must live corruptly or sink beneath a corruption from which we can never hope to rise.

'I think we should go back to the Centre now,' was what he said, in a thin, wavering voice.

They walked back without speaking, entered the side door and found their way through the darkness to the room, where Tom lit a paraffin lamp kept for emergencies. For four hours they sat in silence, Tom in a state of repose; Hugo in turmoil, phrasing endless questions which he never dared voice. When dawn flicked through the high windows, Tom opened his eyes and suggested that they take a walk around the perimeter.

The air was silent and eerie, the sky streaked with a multiplicity of colour like the rainbow at the world's end. A solitary policeman stood near the gate, his jacket unbuttoned, dragging on a cigarette with an air of tiredness or boredom. He did not respond as they approached.

Hugo's foot connected with something in the grass and, looking down, he saw a watch. Bending to pick it up, he noticed a diamond ring nearby. Instinctively he palmed and pocketed this while picking up the watch, which he showed to Tom. As he had foreseen, Tom took the watch and walked toward the policeman.

'Excuse me, sir. Someone has dropped this watch. I think it may have been stolen last night.'

The policeman examined it contemptuously and returned it to Tom.

'Fucking cheap rubbish. Only good for niggers.' He pulled up his sleeve. 'Look, I got four good ones here. You can have that one.'

Hugo stared at the ground with embarrassment as Tom walked back to him. Several more rings and watches lay in the grass. He suddenly realised what had happened. Police had been driving looters down the alleyway then ambushing them, forcing them to jettison their spoils over the fence. Along the length of the alleyway small bright objects glistened in the grass as far as the eye could see.

'Look Tom, the ground is littered with this stuff. Hadn't we better pick it up?'

Tom nodded and produced a plastic carrier bag from his coat pocket. Together they began picking, Tom with the dignified manner of a village crop-planter, Hugo scrambling, rushing every minute to put a fresh handful into Tom's bag. The lack of sleep hit him, he grabbed for jewels which were not there; even when they were he could not rid himself of the sense that he was dreaming. His mind raced like the A train he and Terri would take, debts cleared, all the stuff shifted through her jeweller uncles in Amsterdam, no problem there, the A train to Harlem, to the club where his talent would finally out.

They reached the end of the perimeter. The bag was more than half full.

'I think we should take this stuff in, Tom,' Hugo suggested casually.

'In?'

'Yes. Into the Centre. Quick. Out of the way.'

A pained expressed crossed Tom's face. 'But Hugo. It is stolen. We must take it to the police.'

Hugo sighed. 'Don't you see it's no use? They don't know who it belonged to or where it came from, even if they could be bothered to find out. You saw that copper with his stolen watches. Do you really think they'd return the stuff? Anyway the shops are insured. Nobody will lose.'

Tom threw back his head and closed his eyes. He opened his mouth and took deep breaths of seemingly interminable length.

'You are right.'

Relief swept Hugo: he clasped his hands with joy.

'You are right, Hugo. It is no use giving it to the police for they are as corrupt as those who stole it in the first place. It came from the mouth of the jackal,' his arm arching upward to shoulder height, 'so let it return to the jackal.'

The bag flew up like a slingshot, paused a second in mid-air, then fell in the alley beyond the perimeter fence.

'For God's sake Tom. If you didn't want your half you could have given it to the Order.'

Tom smiled wanly and took Hugo by the shoulder. It was the headmaster routine again.

'Hugo, nothing good can come from money which has been tainted. It would not make them happy, it would not make me happy, it would not make you happy. Come, let's go and have some tea.'

Hugo allowed himself to be led meekly back into the Centre. The solitary copper watched them, his jaded interest tickled by this strange tableau. When they got inside, Tom made the tea while Hugo tried to rationalise what had happened. Pretend it never happened. That was it. They hadn't picked up a mountain of jewellery and thrown it away. They hadn't even left the building. It had all been one big fantasy like winning the pools or getting a legacy from an unknown uncle in Australia. It never happened. It never happened. It never happened.

Tom gave him tea, strong, milkless and sweet, as he always

drank it. They sat in silence. Presently he rose and, separating his papers, put some in front of Hugo.

'I am going to be alone for a while. The Order has sent your first lessons. You can read them if you like.' He moved toward the door and then looked back.

'I warned you Hugo. You would be tested.'

His footsteps retreated down the corridor. Hugo sat, his eyes shut for a long time, until he was completely sure that it had never happened. Then he opened his eyes and looked at his first book of lessons.

Five minutes later he laid down the sheaf of papers and banged his fist several times on the table. He got up, paced the room and kicked the locker. In spite of it all he found it within himself to force a bitter smile. 'Ever bin 'ad, ever bin 'ad, ever bin 'ad,' squawked some spectral parakeet behind his shoulder. It was not that the tablets passed down by the Cosmic Masters were abstruse beyond his comprehension. He could picture their target audience; elderly, predominantly female, distinctly spinsterish, given to divination by tea leaves; compulsive horoscope readers, footlers with the ouija board through which they spoke to Red Indian chieftains and ancient Egyptians. 'Light a candle and stare into the flame. Breathe deeply until the aura changes to blue.' What had been going on over the last month? What spell had be been under to let everything drift on the rocks for this? And those illustrations! You could always tell the loony-tune outfits from their illustrations: yea, by their art-works shall ye know them. The sci-fi kitsch of the Scientologists, the bearded sage of the Rosicrucians offering mail order enlightenment among the incontinence and psoriasis cures, the Jehovah's Witness post-Millennial man dancing in a fair-isle sweater over a sunlit hill where a lion snuggles down with a lamb, and all the lesser examples bedecking the pages of *Old Moore's Almanac*. He picked up the booklet and examined the back. 'The Society of Occultists Ltd,' it announced. One might ask why the Lords of Time, Space and Infinity needed limited liability when they charged twenty quid for this bilge.

It had happened. It had happened. It had happened. The

thought of the small fortune he had allowed to be cast away suddenly broke through his fury. A supermarket bag in the detritus of a riot just, might, dare he hope, dare he think, still be there.

His feet thundered down the corridor, his mind racing, praying that he would not meet Tom, that he would not have to explain himself. Outside the lurid sky had transmuted to piercing blue and the solitary copper had vanished. The rioters and looters were all abed in the hollow under the hill. It would be there, he told himself, walking casually to the gate, out, and down the alley. Yes, Yes! YES, YES, YES, YES, YES, YES:. He could see it; the red, green gold of Krazy Kuts or Kutprice Korner or Kut-U-Like or Kut-the-Krap or whatever-it-was-called, that pile 'em cheap and sell 'em high joint just past Kennington Tube.

He stooped, opening his coat in the manner of a shoplifter and swept the bag under his arm. It felt empty. It was empty. He looked inside, three or four times in case he had missed something, then threw the bag down.

He returned to the gate where the bent copper had stood, sat on an oil drum and cradled his head in his hands. It must have been the copper, who had seen it all. Or it was Tom, who wanted the lot for himself to set up an academy for old lady table-rappers. Or it had been some late rioter drifting home alone and disconsolate, full of the melancholy when the party's over, who had found that some kind gentleman had gift-wrapped a whole parcel of goodies just for him. It had not been Hugo James. Dully he remembered the ring which he had palmed into his pocket, and searched, but found nothing. Perhaps he had put it in with the rest.

But then it had never happened had it? Keep saying it. It never happened. It never happened. It never happened.

A wind blew up carrying a smell of burning, the whiff of some doused-down building yielding its last breath of smoke to the sky. Cars were moving somewhere. It was about the time that people went to work. A strange wind, an African wind; a strange smell, of a village at morning; a strange image of a small white boy imbibing holy writ from a black master. The enemy, whatever it had been, was no longer near.

Hugo opened his eyes and looked up but the wind blew dust or smoke or whatever in them. Blinking, he thought he saw a figure, tall, dignified, black, standing at the great window: the whole building seemed to shake with laughter as his eyelids flickered. When he could see properly, the figure, if it had been there at all, had gone.

'I warned you Hugo. You will be tested.'

Those had been Tom's last words to him. No exaggeration there. He couldn't face Tom now, nor tomorrow night, nor ever again. There was nothing in the Centre he wanted except his bicycle, padlocked just inside the door.

As he cycled through Brixton, the blue had taken over the streets again except for a few shopkeepers sweeping up or counting the cost. Boards were going up over broken windows everywhere, the knock of hammers like jungle drums. If he cycled fast, he might just meet the postman at Peckham Rye, bearing down on his house with a fresh sack of woe.

ALEX BARR

The Fan

She had caught him out in an affair, and now they were starting again. They walked through the woods talking of travel. The woods were a tame strip between houses and a golf course, and down by the brook, where new sewers had been laid, new saplings were just beginning to add height.

She said, 'We could go to Canada for a year. You could work there.'

She thought it would be a relief to be far from the other woman. Even now the woman's husband would phone her to ask angrily why she hadn't prevented it. She tried to explain that she and her husband had no authority over one another, that she could never be sure what he was thinking.

She repeated, 'Do you fancy Canada?'

He thought of the song *The Green Fields of Canada*, the young Irishman's farewell to his home, and a tear came into his eye. He wiped it away hastily, as if it were an insect, so she wouldn't notice.

He said, 'Possibly. I thought of somewhere more exotic.'

'Where?'

He didn't know. Somewhere with stars he could lie and look at, without street lights. Where he could lose himself in a profound blackness, the earth warm under him. A desert perhaps. He knew if he said this his wife would say, 'All right, a desert,' and he'd have to list possible names, consult the atlas. So he said nothing.

She said, not one to give up easily, 'Canada's interesting.'

He asked, 'But what would *you* do?'

'Get some kind of job. Anything. The children could easily go to school there.'

They walked in silence for a while. Over their heads a squirrel leapt from one tree to another, showering ash keys. She took his hand and rubbed it, as if trying to bring him back to life. Since he gave up the other woman he's been empty of feeling. She too was empty now, her anger all burned out.

She held his hand against her hip as they walked, and he felt a quiver of desire, as if his skin ached. He would have liked them to slither halfway down to the brook and make love among the rhododendrons, but he feared she'd ask whether he'd been here with the other woman. He had not. They walked on.
She asked, 'What do you think?'
'I'd really imagined going abroad alone.'
She kept hold of his hand, because that had become part of the rhythm of the walk, but her chest and stomach felt suddenly cold, encapsulated, as if she were a vacuum flask.

He never expected the affair to work. He knew it was doomed, that there would be much more pain than pleasure. But without pain there would be no art, no *Tosca*, no *Tristan and Isolde*. He'd read only weeks before, as if fate were preparing him for the encounter, about the 'unassailable soul of the warrior', and elsewhere, about following love whenever called, 'even though you know he will wound you'. When he stood in the school orchestra pit smelling of old timber and dust, and the woman, sewing in the wings, looked down at him with smouldering eyes, he could not deny himself to her.
He was conducting his Opus Three, *Overture and Incidental Music to The Real King Arthur*. The play, comparing history with legend, had been written by his daughter's English teacher. The woman, whose children were also at the high school, had designed the costumes.
Biting a thread, she joked, 'Only Opus Three? At your age?'
'I'm a late starter.'
'Well at least you won't peak too early.'
He found that his daughter considered her smarmy and overbearing. By this time they were starting the affair, and as his daughter suspected nothing he thought it tactically wise to agree.
The affair was brief. His wife was more perceptive than he'd realised. He thought she'd fail to notice his extra hours at rehearsal, and he was right. But he hadn't allowed for her noticing his erratic changes of mood, the hours he sat dreamily at the piano. In the messy aftermath, his wife and the woman's husband picked through the rubble like fire investigators. The woman asked

him to pretend to give her up but go on seeing her in secret. He refused. He also refused to hide from his wife the fact that she still phoned him. She cried, but respected him. But when she heard of his daughter's remark, and his full agreement with it, she felt betrayed and her respect evaporated. She wrote to say she detested him, his way of life, and most of all, his music.

She receded into his past, a ghost he sometimes saw when the coach returned their children from school trips. The pain from such sightings, from the knowledge of what she now thought of him, he bore almost with pride. He'd prepared for the worst. He had the unassailable soul of the warrior. Besides the suffering would feed his art. The woman was his Mathilde Wesendonck, his wife was his Cosima. Of course, the comparisons with Wagner were inexact. For example, Wagner would have scorned the school orchestra pit as acoustically disastrous.

What was harder to bear was his wife's pain. The way she scraped and scraped at the wood of cupboards for hours to strip them, then collapsed into a chair, too drained even to watch TV or put on music. It was a dull, uninspiring stoicism. He preferred the blazing anger she'd shown when she first found out and they fought like animals, she tearing at his face and lunging at his testicles, he pinning her wrists and roaring at her. These encounters would often end with their pulling each other's clothes off and making love with intense relief. But when, soon after the walk in the woods, a kind of fog came down between them, he felt oppressed by their life. There was nothing noble about it. Their quarrels were trivial, about spilt jam, socks the children lost. In the library of the college where he worked was a handbook of the world's higher education. He began to browse in it after work, and write letters asking for one-year appointments.

His wife, who in the past had not noticed discrepancies in his timing, now thought he might be seeing the woman again. She wondered how to be sure. He seemed withdrawn and preoccupied, but that could be work, or her own shut-down state. It wasn't in her to spy, go through his pockets, or wait and watch, on her days off, in the café across the road from his department. Besides, she'd rather live with uncertainty than know the answer, because if the answer was Yes, it would be the end.

Nevertheless, she couldn't help commenting on his lateness.

He said, 'I'm just spending time in the library.'

'Doing what?'

He was unwilling to tell her about the applications. If they came to nothing he's feel small in her eyes. 'Research.'

'On what?' Not meaning to test him now, simply wanting to be reassured that they could still talk. About anything, the more down-to-earth the better. If he wanted to let off steam about work, that was fine, then she could do the same. Except that there was no steam inside her, only ice. She smiled wryly at the image, his steam melting her ice.

He asked, 'What are you smiling at? Don't you believe me? I'm researching the life of Wagner.'

He thought that a convenient subject, since he already knew so much, and she wasn't aware how much he knew.

She said, 'Tell me about it.' She thought, Tell me anything, anything you think or feel.

He told her Wagner's life was like a fairy tale: nearly drowned at sea escaping from a dull routine, dogged by failure in Paris, never losing faith in his vision, rescued at last from poverty by King Ludwig of Bavaria. Soothed by Cosima. He omitted any mention of Mathilde.

She asked, 'And what will you compose next? What's Opus Four?'

He shrugged. He distrusted the subject. He had some disjointed themes in his head, which he would have liked to play to get her reaction, but he feared they would skip back into discussing Opus Three, inseparable from the school play and the other woman. She might ask again, as she'd asked so often. 'But why? Why did you do it?' And when he failed to reply, 'Admit it, I bored you, you wanted to fuck somebody different, a different body.' Making him seem crude and self-seeking. Not someone who simply gave of himself. Not someone prepared to pluck the *Heidenröslein* and be lacerated with thorns.

The Fan

He received a letter from the University of Omdurman. Yes, they would employ him for a year, to develop a course in acoustics, the physics of music, the mathematics of harmony. The name Omdurman excited him. The scene of the last cavalry charge, in which the youthful Winston Churchill had taken part. A city of traders in gold, at the meeting of two great rivers. He brought the letter home, smiling.

His wife said, 'I didn't know you were writing letters.'

He played down his having applied, and spoke enthusiastically about his head of department's web of foreign contacts. His wife was left with the impression that he hadn't so much sought this offer as had it thrust upon him. She knew nothing of Omdurman. They looked at the map together. Her husband seemed to know what it would be like there, tracing the two rivers with his finger, the finger that had secretly touched the other woman. But she received no impression except, from the climate graph, one of heat.

She said, 'Good. When do we go?'

She thought he seemed surprised by her willingness.

'July.'

The University had enclosed some fact sheets, which didn't seem to interest her husband. She went through them carefully, trying to decide what clothes to take, what injections were needed, where the children would go to school. She asked him to check how much of his salary he would be able to send home, and at what rate of exchange. They could let the house for a year, but the rest might only just cover the mortgage, and they had other payments to keep up.

The more she read about education, the more uneasy she became. There were only Islamic schools, and one private college run by Jesuit priests. The older child was about to choose her GCSE subjects, the younger was struggling with his maths. She wanted them to be happy, to have successful lives. They weren't too happy now because of the emotional fog inside their home, but at least they could look forward to careers, and supportive partners.

She said, 'I don't think we can go.'

Her husband stared at her, his mouth trying to form a reply. She explained at length about education. He went for a long walk, looking all round him at the fields, at the distant houses and still more distant hills, as if for something he'd lost. When he returned it was dark. The stars were obscured by cloud. The children were going through their bedtime rituals, which absorbed all his wife's attention. When they'd settled they looked at one another, each trying to read the other's face.

She said, 'Perhaps *you* should go.'

His heart leapt. He said, 'Without you? No.'

'But it's what you wanted.'

'When I said that . . .' He shrugged. He'd been about to continue, 'I was confused,' but that would have been a gross lie. The pain had given him a sense of clarity, of living deeply. It was now, when the pain had dulled, that he felt confused. He said, 'I don't know, I don't know.'

In the end he decided to go. It would enliven his CV. It could even be a good career move. The music of another continent could inspire and inform his Opus Four. In the desert, away from street lights, he'd see more stars than he'd believed possible. As for money, he'd be able to send a proportion home: he'd checked that with the consulate. The exchange rate was poor, and of course his UK salary would be suspended, but his wife assured him that she'd manage. There was just enough, and it was only for a year. Meanwhile the University would pay for one return flight home, and one return flight for his family to Omdurman. After he'd settled in, they'd come for a few weeks' holiday.

The night before he was to leave, in bed, his wife cried. She realised she hadn't quite believed he would go alone. She went over the past few years and thought how things ought to have been. She thought how other families, their friends, lingered over meals together, played ball games in their gardens. Her husband asked what was wrong.

'I feel abandoned.'

He said, 'I could still not go.' He wondered whether, if she leapt at this, he'd feel frustration or relief.

'Your decision's made. I wouldn't respect you now if you didn't go.'

The Fan

He dabbed at her tears, trying not to cry himself. The books he'd read before his affair, about the path of the warrior, about love, hadn't mentioned this kind of situation. He felt his resolve in danger. For months the fog had stopped his wife's words and feelings touching him deeply. Later when she fell asleep he looked at her face, which suddenly looked unfamiliar. When next he saw her she would look even more strange. He sought for a form of words that would carry him through. He thought, This is what I wanted. No, this is what I'm fated to do. The thoughts made him feel no different. He hummed to himself the Prelude to Act One of *Lohengrin*. The music warmed his heart, and after a while he too slept.

The journey to London seemed ordinary. The train, the scenery were pleasantly familiar. The idea that he was taking a flight alone seemed unreal. When he'd flown before it had always been with his wife and children on holidays, or on rare academic trips with colleagues. It was only when he got off the Tube that he felt his real journey begin. He was staying with friends who lived half a mile from the Tube station, too close for it to be worth taking a cab. He moved his four heavy pieces of luggage two at a time, walking ten paces with the first two, going back for the second two, walking forward till all four pieces were reunited, then repeating the process. Sweating freely, he submitted himself to the discipline. He noticed that when his luggage was at its greatest separation, he felt anxious, but that the anxiety diminished as it came back together.

In the morning, once again it was hard to believe he was going. His friends usually drove him to the main-line station for a train home. When they drove to Heathrow he almost called out that they'd taken a wrong turning. But at the airport he was reassured, because by the check-in desk were the most handsome people he'd ever seen. Three men, very tall, with high domed foreheads and finely sculptured faces, their skin a rich, slightly dusty black. On their wiry night-black hair sat delicate round skullcaps of white openwork. Two women, wide-eyed, attractive, their heads covered by white shawls of surprising delicacy and lightness. His heart lifted on seeing them. It was clear he was taking the right step, going to a land of people such as these.

Walking to the plane he had a moment of doubt. There were other aircraft, from India, the Far East, Australasia. Was he going to the right continent after all? Was it possible that his destiny lay elsewhere, that he'd somehow misread the signals? But here were the steps, his feet were leaving the surface of his homeland, now visible either side of the handrail, grey, crisscrossed by tubes and cables.

His was a middle seat, facing a pale grey bulkhead with a mural of flying storks. In the window seat on his right was another of the men with fine black features, but rather smaller and slighter. In the aisle seat, a bulky man who greeted him.

'Hi there. They don't give us a hell of a lot of space.'

They smiled at one another. He wondered whether he should have perhaps gone to America. The fellow was so relaxed and confident. The man by the porthole was more formal. He seemed to have no English. They nodded politely to one another. Well, soon he'd be able to address these people in their own tongue. After the first meal was cleared away, against the steady throb of the engines, he studied the language book.

The poor man, where is his house? — Sir, I do not know.
Is the road long? — Yes, the road is very long indeed.
O girl, mother of big earrings —

He closed the book. He would not be speaking to women, not socially, not alone. To go through the pain of abandoning the other woman, only to fall into the same trap in Omdurman through sheer loneliness, would be cosmic joke.

He closed his eyes and put on the headphones; alien music filtered through him washing away the past. A new beginning, a new beginning. The singer's voice hesitated and soared in quarter-tones, and a flock of string instruments, like a flock of evening swifts, hesitated and soared with him, while a drum like a sleeper's pulse beat gently and artfully. He settled into his seat. Perhaps this new stream would flow into his own compositions. As Wagner had transcended the narrow rivalries of German and Italian opera, had forged a new whole on the anvil of his suffering, he would bring Omdurman home, or home to Omdurman.

A journey of peace. – And you Sir, God give you peace.

He dozed as the plane beat southwards.

When drinks came the American asked where he was headed. He explained about the University. The American said every rainy season some part of the one railroad from port to capital was washed away, blocking the flow of food and raw material.

'That's when they turn to air freight. Which is where I come in.'

With his big face and wide shoulders, the man had the air of someone not very important in his own right, but useful as part of a greater whole. Another voice in the chorus, two more hands to the pump. He kept twisting in his seat.

'My goddamn back. Injured it years ago.'

'So what do you do on long flights?'

The man grinned. 'Suffer, what else? In the hotel I'll run a bath, hot as I dare, and lower myself in. Fwsssh! And you? Which hotel are you in?'

'Don't know yet. Being met, by the University.'

Later, after crossing a new coastline, he spoke to the man on his right.

'Where are you going?'

'El Obeid.'

'What is it like, El Obeid?'

'It is my home.'

They smiled, and again nodded politely. Beyond the man's shoulder, through the porthole, the sunset was a fiery brushstroke on the horizon. He thought

The lone and level sands stretch far away

and spent a dreamy half hour trying vainly to remember where the line came from. At least now he could write to his wife and children. *I watched the sun set behind the desert.* The brushstroke faded. Night fell.

When the aircraft rolled to a halt he felt tense until the doors were opened. The air outside had a burnt smell, like clods of couch-grass on a slow bonfire. He filled in an immigration form on poor quality paper, irritated by the delay, then filed past a control kiosk. A man with stars on his shoulder-straps took the form and stamped his passport. The man's face, dark brown rather than black, was pitted as if from smallpox. He went through, found his luggage, all four pieces intact, and pressed on to the arrivals hall.

He stood on tiptoe, looking above the crowd for a placard bearing his name. He felt that once he saw it, in this echoing space, something would have been proved, something settled. It was like a photographic negative of the departure lounge. Now he and the other Europeans were the exotic ones, weaving in and out of the crowd of black men like figures from someone's dream. There was no sign of the tall fine-looking men and handsome women he'd seen at the check-in. Perhaps they were already halfway home. The crowd thinned: he no longer had to stretch. No-one held a placard, with his name or any other. When only officials, police, and baggage-handlers were left he knew he was alone.

At a small kiosk, so dimly lit that at first he thought it closed, he changed his cash for local currency. He thrust into his back pocket the foreign notes, limp and greasy from numberless sweaty hands, and looked for a taxi. Outside, in the profound dark beyond the lights of the building, men in voluminous white turbans and white robes like nightshirts flitted like moths, like spectres. Above him were the stars, intense and numerous; he paused for a moment to look up, but after a moment anxiety drove him on. To his great relief, in the taxi queue he found the American.

He said, 'No-one came.'

The American shrugged with a wry smile, as if to say, What did you expect? They waited together. In front he heard British voices, someone talking about econometrics.

He said, 'Excuse me, do you work at the University?'

The fellow turned, and before nodding studied his face and clothes.

He went on. 'I should have been met. No-one came. Where does one stay?'

The fellow looked at him vacantly. 'Where you like. We're going to sleep on a friend's roof.'

Someone else said, 'The University uses the Hotel Percival.'

The Fan

He shared a taxi with the American, who pointed out, under a concrete road bridge, the meeting of the two rivers. He wondered whether his wife and children would enjoy, after all, a holiday here. The American was dropped at the Grand, a reassuring building with floodlit flags on stainless-steel masts, still full of visible activity despite the hour. The English names, Grand, Percival, were reassuring. After all, the place wasn't that foreign, it was only a few decades after the end of British rule.

The Percival was almost in darkness, occupying half a block. The city-centre blocks were hard-edged and rectilinear. Opposite the hotel, at ground floor level, was a row of galvanised steel shutters in a framework of concrete columns. Inside, the small reception lobby was lit by a yellow bulb and smelt of fenugreek, cigarettes, and hot dusty leather. A porter, small, thin-faced, rather frail, his skin grey rather than black, showed him to the fourth floor. Their slow steps echoed on the terrazzo. Each carried two pieces of luggage.

The room was a normal hotel room, if a little severe. A bed, a window, a ceiling fan. On the tiled floor near the window, traces of sand. He pulled back the curtain, exposing a door to a balcony. It faced a concrete building a few yards away. He went out, treading unevenly on more sand, and saw on his right the shuttered building across the street. A car drove by, its headlights dim, the beams a little misty, slowing and beeping at the intersection.

The porter, examining the coin he had been given, left him. He stripped off his shirt, and in the small ensuite splashed cold water over the sweat of his chest and stomach. He ignored his back, which when he lay on the bed stuck to the sheet. A small black beetle travelled intently across the floor. A fly buzzed in a corner. He watched them with relief: at least it was no worse, these were the only signs of life. Above him the fan beat slowly, the shadows of the blades sliding across the wall in a giant dance. He was here, in a room in Omdurman, scene of the last cavalry charge, a city where gold was wrought.

The fan turned with a rhythm which seemed to hesitate. He tried to fit a tune to it. The Prelude to Act One of *Lohengrin* seemed to fit if he increased the tempo, but as it reached its climax, the clash of cymbals, broke away completely. He realised it had never really fitted, that beneath the apparent fluidity of the music, the liquid, molten notes, was a firm unyielding pulse. He tried his own Opus Three. It brought back the smell of the school hall, of the orchestra pit. He thought it would bring back the other woman, grinning at him from over her sewing, but what came was the sight of his children walking towards him in their blazers across the dusty maple flooring. The fan blurred and jumped as his eyes filled with tears. He wiped them and hummed *My Funny Valentine*. That brought back his wife's single bed in her student flat, the pillow with the light fragrance of her hair. He remembered the alien landscape of her body, the giddy sensation when they embraced naked, sweating in the midsummer heat. The fan would not fit *My Funny Valentine*, which came in sallies, in flurries, like the music of *Tristan*, not in a steady thrum-thrum-thrum.

He thought of the money he'd send to his wife, his first pay cheque. Did the University know he existed? His name had not appeared on a white card. But tomorrow he could collect his Initial Payment. Meanwhile the cash he'd changed would last. He was wise not to bring a cheque book or traveller's cheques, so as not to drain the home finances. He wife would just manage till he started to send his pay. With a sudden rush of anxiety he rolled off the narrow bed and reached for his trousers.

He took the dull-textured wad from the back pocket and spread it on the fibre-board bedside table. The rate of exchange was wrong. He'd been cheated. But no, here was the transaction slip, headed in alien script but also in English, the official airport bureau de change. The rate was clearly stated. What he had left, allowing for the taxi fare, was correct. Since he'd first inquired the rate had changed. Or he'd been told wrong. No, it must have changed, the economies of these countries were notoriously unstable. His university salary would convert at a tenth of what he'd believed.

He calculated, with an unsteady heartbeat, the amount he could send home to his wife. It was laughable, hardly worth the commission he'd pay to convert and send it. What would she say?

The Fan

You who are called my husband, have you yet again deceived me? — I was led astray.

He stretched on the bed again and watched the fan. He had abandoned any thought of music. It was night. The hotel was quiet. He had no sense of time, his watch was beside the window. He watched the blades turn, just fast enough to blur the edges of the blades, and the edge of the shadow of each blade as it slid across the wall. The beetle crossed the floor, skirting his shoe, the sign of an immense life the beetle could not conceive of. He thought of Wagner, penniless in Paris having quit his dull job in Riga. His failures, exile, loss of Mathilde, impoverished trek from town to town. Then the knock at the door, the fairytale messenger from King Ludwig, the glorious rescue. The fan continued to turn in the breathless hush of the hotel. He heard distant steps in the corridor and listened as they died away. The blades of the fan, the chrome central boss, moved endlessly, with occasional hesitations. Only his reflection in the chrome, greyish-pink on the grey-white bed, was motionless, unbelievably small.

WILLIAM CAMPBELL

Change at Crewe

The woman's arm eased into the right sleeve of Lawrence's discarded shirt. Its unrestrained movement reminded him of the pain in his triceps. Her reflection arched in the wall-mirror as she sought the left armhole, breasts flattened by the Lycra singlet she had produced from her shoulder-bag. Her Aladdin's cave, he thought.

His shirt. What next. Lawrence wondered, trepidant, terrified, still with his aching erection.

He caught his own face close to in the mirror of the toilet, the packaging tape a beige clinical mask across his mouth. Not across his nose. She had taunted him with that for twenty-three seconds, counting aloud each one elephant, two elephant, her at-the-circus eyes staring at him until he was on the point of vomiting. The instant she stripped his nose free his hatred flipped to benediction. He would have done anything she asked.

That was just after Crewe, soon after the prolonged clatter of bogeys over points and the lurch of the carriage as it crossed other tracks prevented anyone hearing his shriek. One cry was all he got out, from the back of his throat, no power in it. Then the tape, fifty millimetres wide, squashed his face from left to right, tightly wound from behind. Packaging tape from the shoulder-bag.

Emily finished buttoning his shirt, top to bottom, fumbling with left-over-right unfamiliarity, reversed in the mirror, he noticed.

'Say byesie-byesie to my tits, lover.' She bounced her chest into his back, adding her weight for a moment to Lawrence's crucifix arms. Arms screaming with the agony of suspending his own weight. He knew from experience it was well over an hour to London. He groaned behind the gag. He remembered the absence of nail-varnish against the white of his shirt. She had peeled off the crimson points and secreted them in her bag. Her wig of short blond waves sat on the vanity shelf in front of the frosted window.

She stepped into his trousers and pulled them over her hips. A

Change at Crewe

flush of shame hit Lawrence. What if she had not locked the door? A passenger could enter, see him naked with this woman dressed as a man. What would they think? Or the ticket inspector. Lawrence peered down his nose trying to see the bolt of the lock in the mirror. He tried to straighten his neck. His head was clamped backwards over his shoulder blades by packaging tape, a long olive scarf and his own belt. The leather bound his ankles, doubled up behind him. Her innovation had excited him after the first bruising shock.

Privacy. It became vital to check the toilet was locked no matter what pains stabbed from his bonds. He could not move his head, the crêpe scarf gave nothing. Each tug made his pinched cervical vertebrae jab him sharply.

Emily had her back to him, adjusting the knot of his tie at her larynx. She was leaning over the wash basin, glancing at him from time to time in the basin mirror with the same distracted amusement he had noticed on the platform at Carlisle. She had paced it like a zoo lioness, an unprepossessing long fawn coat, a flange of olive, black loafers, to and fro in front of him. Shearing his line of vision. She stopping to look up the track, he stared down the platform.

She paced again, passed in front of him. Same height as him, square chin, late forties craw, etched eyes, no ring. He would fuck her and at Euston forget her. Carlisle, Oxenholme, Preston, the ticket inspection then non-stop to Euston.

'Did the station announcer say the London train was forty, four-o minutes late?' She stopped her return pass along the platform and looked at him with a neutral face not quite concealing interest. He thought she had not understood the point of his question, the verbalised point. 'Earlier, he was so particular to say only fourteen, one-four minutes late.'

'Yes. Fourteen, then twenty-two, then forty.' A quiet voice, slowly releasing the words. He could clearly hear her over the echoing clatter of station activity. Her gaze darted over his face, never lingering long enough to be caught, totting the information.

'Much more delay and we'll be catching the train that's gone.' Spoken without a smile so he restrained his laugh. Now her eyes roved down his body. He twitched involuntarily but he was confident she had not detected it.

'In that case I'm having a coffee. Want to join me?'

He watched the ash face turn to an undistinguished profile as the woman brushed by him, stepping directly towards the *Travellers Fare* snack bar as if he were not there. Lawrence glimpsed the curve of breast veiled by dainty blouse as her coat momentarily gaped. He reckoned she had let this happen, he was into recognising all the come-on tricks from shy women. For a second he smelt the trace of heavy perfume, unusual for daytime.

He bought the coffees and she asked about his job. He told her of his many responsibilities, let his sales patter work for him not for the company this time.

'Does your wife mind you being away so much?'

'I'm not married.'

She knew he lied. He was too easy in the company of a woman, not over-quick in word or action from a desperate hunger. She slipped her coat off her shoulders to hang from the back of the plastic chair. A different hunger slid across his lips when her blouse tightened from the movement. She told him she was divorced.

'Children?' he asked.

She did not immediately answer. He saw her thoughts roll along the railway track, a gentle curve leaving the platform, the sleepers more grassed as they vanished from the station. They weaved through picturesque countryside and terminated in the Glasgow tumult.

'No,' she answered, too firmly.

'Wish you did?' he said after a pause. He had checked himself from saying wish you had. Reminding her of time gone, biological clocks, could make her hostile to him and the plans he had for her.

'No. It would be a nightmare naming them.'

'That's as good a reason as any I suppose.'

'Names shape a person's character,' she retorted. 'Make them who they are. Nicknames, hate-names, make-you-cry names, make-me-friend names.'

'What's yours?' he asked, surprised at the emotion in her voice.

'We are what we are named. We have no choice. Parents inflict the label on us. Damn them.'

'Mine's Lawrence.' Her voice had become loud, drawing attention. She noticed Lawrence's embarrassment.

'How do they know who we really are?' she said softly.

She drank some coffee, keeping the cup to her lips, peering at him over the cup. Mummy was inspecting him: cap straight, blazer pockets empty, bus fare safe. And later: sandwiches in brief-case, season ticket in top pocket, don't stay late at the office – I've got your favourite tea, you mind those flighty secretaries.

'That's an okay name, I suppose. I detest being Emily.'

'Perhaps I can help you forget who you are for a while.' His shoe brushed her calf under the table and he was pleased she did not pull her leg away.

Emily back-kicked him in the kidney. The lock on the toilet door was jolted from his thoughts. His brogue on her foot heeled into his soft flesh, make him jiggle like a puppet.

'Don't get impatient. There's lots more fun yet.' Emily resumed the careful removal of her make-up.

She was excellent at kicks. Like a rocket, the power from every muscle pushing against some launch pad, explosively propelled through femur and tibia. Lawrence had seen her grip the edge of the basin, flatten her stomach against it and suddenly he was all pain.

Over the points at Crewe he had seen nothing coming. Tied and stretched across the small cubicle he was still in control. She had been permitted to do this – by him.

In the tiny room he had started by caressing her thighs, kissed the cool flesh, unhooked twelve-denier charcoal and rolled one down to her toes. Then its partner.

'Shall we try something a bit different this time?' she asked. We, partner, sharing thrills, collusive sex. She wanted to please him; she would not be a woman to teach or to scold him. He had known from the way she paced the platform he had chosen the right woman.

This second time in the toilet with Emily would not be like Oxenholme to Preston – frenetic, quick, hair unruffled. Straighten skirt, zip-up, nothing said until they returned to their facing seats with a table between. And after Preston, after the ticket inspection, she had responded to his stroking enquiry with her foot, slipped out of its loafer. He registered her initiative and he felt good. Lawrence had screwed liveliness into the woman and now he would have real fun. They had separately gone to the same toilet, the nearest with no passengers to observe entries and exists.

'Different? Anything you want,' he had answered.

She coaxed him out of jacket and shirt with tentative, wandering hands. Smiling, kind, she tied the end of a stocking round each of Lawrence's wrists. Mummy slid the woollen gloves over his hands and coaxed down the finger stalls. Looking at him from time to time, Emily carefully formed the knots without hurry. Efficient, ungiving clove-hitches. He felt the pulse in his swelling hands, an urgency in his groin.

'I was in the Brownies,' she explained.

Emily faced him towards the large wall-mirror across the toilet from the door and the wash-basin. She meticulously fastened one wrist to the top of the vertical grab-rail to the left of the mirror, securing the remainder of the stocking round the horizontal metal bar across the window.

'We don't want you slipping down, do we?' Her hand brushed the front of his trousers. Lawrence gasped. He heard Warrington swish by outside the frosted window.

She took his right arm with the same slow ritual, raising the wrist to the large coat-hook high on the corridor wall. Royal blue plastic, right angled with a finial too wide for any garment hook to slide over. Or for a bound wrist to slide free.

Lawrence was stretched in two. Tethered across the toilet, this woman had the opportunity to do anything she wanted to him. He knew she could, emphasised by the pinching restraints on his wrists and a growing ache in his right shoulder. Deep beneath his short-breath excitement he knew she would not. They never did.

It was his game and he was the ring-master and the expert. It was he who had selected her, had her between Oxenholme and Preston, teased her under the table in the open carriage and drew her into playing his game. He was late from work; your tea is ruined, she scolded, I made it specially for you; guilty for upsetting her, resentful against being made to feel bad about mummy.

Emily played his game well. Nearing Crewe she had him undressed and made him crazy with her touches. She sat splay-legged on the basin, skirt rumpled across her belly, glueing his eyes to her nudity.

'This what you want? You got to want it real bad this time, lover.' He did, he did. He groaned.

'Does Emily please you?' She gripped the basin surround, raised her hips and gyrated her pelvis. Lawrence was mesmerised. Emily's body began bobbing to the clatter of the points.

She kicked. Launched herself at him. Both feet rammed into the small of Lawrence's back. He was flattened against the mirror, winded. Emily kicked again. She levered power from the wall at her back. Breath was pummelled from him. Steam-hammer action. He tried to gulp for air but the continual kicking panicked him.

Emily slipped to the floor, looped Lawrence's belt round his ankles and yanked them from under him. He crashed onto his knee-caps. His manacled arms were wrenched from their sockets. One croaked shriek then the gag. The packaging tape to hand from her shoulder bag. He heard the tearing noise unreel round his face, pulled roughly. Ecstatic terror as the mask suffocated. But she had released him into a gasping hard bliss. Before the *Caledonian* had cleared the crossings south of Crewe he was hog-tied feet to head behind his back.

Emily played very well. Lawrence's excitement was intense, flooding his body more comprehensively than for a long time. Strung up. Unpredictable danger yet with the ultimate safety-net – her scruples.

Musky perfume dragged through his nose. He was back on the Carlisle platform. The scent of the chase. Lily of the valley, *Convallaria*. He had genned up on the name. *Diorissimo*. Lawrence bought it for his wife from duty-free shops. She wore it every day.

A heavier perfume, the same essence, rose over his shoulders, choking as exhaust fumes in congested traffic. It overwhelmed the smell of zealous toilet cleanser. Emily had pulled the bottle from her bag. She sprayed him until the mist formed droplets under his arms. She massaged it into his skin, clawing him occasionally on the bare chest, triggering a reaction in his genitals. All the time she talked softly to him, silly talk, rub-a-dub-dub, three men in a tub. He would have to buy another bottle for the wife, tell he it was tomfoolery with the tester and Gerald from the Carlisle office.

Pat-a-cake, pat-a-cake. Emily's hands fluttered down both sides of his body. Tell me the name of your young man. Over his flanks.

'Ready for the grand finale, lover? The climax?' she asked, making light whirlpools on the tensed front of his thighs. Lawrence tried to nod assent.

'Cat got your tongue?' she teased. 'Run rabbit run. Somebody's a-quiver to see me.' A locker-room laugh barked from her. A girlie voice so close in his ear he felt the heat in the breath. 'Georgie Porgie, pudding and pie, kissed the girls and made them cry, made them cry. Bastard.' She bit the lobe. The surprise and the pain were a thrill, quickly gone. He craved for more.

'Neat fit, huh?' Emily paraded herself in the big mirror. She twanged the scarf pinning back his head until he stopped dwelling on himself and looked. Lawrence saw his clothes on her, shirt, tie, suit.

'Do you think I'd make a good Lawrence? Think I could be you?'

Something in the reflection nagged at the back of his mind.

'Time you were dressed, Emily,' she said. A motherly voice, gently urging the boy not to miss the bus to school. Emily was suddenly busy, coaxing his feet into the loafers. There had always been reproof in his mother's voice, no matter what he achieved. If only you had got out of bed earlier, eaten your cereal quicker, an 'A' is all right but an 'A plus' would have been better.

'Have to put you on a diet,' said Emily, fighting the button into the waist-band of the wrap-round skirt. He drew in his stomach, must try to please her. She draped the fullness of material round his flanks, jostling his belted ankles.

'Good job I brought my own belt. What embarrassment if my trousers fell down.' She wrenched her blouse between her hands sending pearl buttons bouncing and rolling across the vinyl floor. She threw the torn blouse onto the floor in front of him.

Change at Crewe

The purposefulness of her action registered with Lawrence. 'My own belt' hopped in and out of his thoughts leaving leaden footprints. She had prepared for this. She had planned to have him tethered across the cubicle. His innards dropped through his guts. Two ring-masters in the game.

The wig was rammed down on Lawrence's head. The movements woke the pincers in the back of his neck, searing away his humiliation at seeing the blond waves squatting on his crown. She had parted her hair on the left, that was what had niggled his memory. It was a man he had seen in the mirror, in his clothes. Himself. She had not been joking about being him. How much of him did she want?

'Actually, I think Lawrence is a rubbish name.' Emily was tucking his hair under the wig. 'It'll have to do for now. All boys' names are rubbish.'

She admired her work like a hairdresser behind her client. 'Girls have pretty names. Some, anyway.'

Emily looped her brassière round his chest, unclipping one fastener of each strap. 'You'll grow into it.' He was always too small for the clothes mummy bought him. Disapproving of his size, though it was mummy who bought them.

'Emily ain't bad. Best name I had was Rowena.' He heard the brush of Emily's shoulder-bag as one hand rummaged. It occurred to him how sharply aware he was of the sound above the clatter of the train.

'She wasn't pretty though. I had to take the name off her. Didn't deserve such a pretty name.'

Thoughts vanished quicker than they arrived, never fully formed. Lawrence speculated what Emily was scrabbling for. Nothing fixed in his mind.

'You thought I was pretty, didn't you. Even though I was Emily. Little Jack Horner, always wanting to stick in your thumb. The apple of every girl's eye, are you?' sang Emily.

Lawrence saw the thing Emily had rummaged for.

'An apple a day keeps the curse away. Oh no it doesn't my pretty maid.'

Twenty centimetres from his nose.

'What's that stain? You disgusting, filthy girl.'

Emily's fingertips held the flat brass handle as if it were a delicate ornament.

'You've ruined another good sheet.'

His heart dropped a beat.

'Dirty, girl. Unclean. Get out of this house.'

Then it was taken from his vision.

'Apple-pie clean. Clean, clean then my Country Cousins won't come.'

He knew exactly the keenness of the blade pressed flat against his penis. Against his vulnerable skin the edge was rasp-rough with its awful potential.

'One rotten apple can spoil the tart. Throw it out. Mess. Spoilt.'

It slightly indented his flesh. He ejaculated.

'Naughty Emily,' chided the woman wearing his clothes. She was the only thing he saw. 'So impatient. We'll have to mop up that nasty, nasty mess.' She made a fuss of looking round the toilet muttering to herself, what shall we use.

A relief had bathed Lawrence's body and mind allowing the pains in his arms and neck to lift like a morning mist. His thoughts raced along the track beside the train, heedless of time and place and direction.

'I know the very thing. Wash away.'

Lawrence wanted to tell her he was not ready for more, not yet. He needed to savour this rapture. A feather tickled his throat. He strained against his tethered head to look down in the mirror and saw its red trail. He watched Emily, now a wide-eyed rabbit caught in headlights, spellbound by the tapestry of her deeds. She moved the handle into a clenched fist, holding it tightly. The line across his throat started to tingle with an oozing curtain of crimson.

Lawrence concentrated on his hands cutting the balsa-wood. He carefully steered the flat brass handle of his *X-Acto* so the blade followed the printed lines marking the fuselage ribs. He wanted so much for it to be right for mummy. Emily's knife only had a common-or-garden razor for its blade. His was a proper scalpel, a crescent blade held in place by a nut and a tiny silver thumb-screw. Emily's was a make-do tomahawk, a *Blue Peter* assembly for an *Action Man* doll. Lawrence smiled.

Emily slashed across his throat. She slashed again, ear to ear. Lawrence was stunned immobile. Again, the razor snagged its square end. He felt her annoyance as she jabbed and twisted it free from the cut. She struck the left carotid artery. A gusher.

Lawrence's heart pumped his life against the mirror. A swelling red octopus dropped tentacles down the glass.

'Disgusting, dirty girl. Mess everywhere.'

Over the octopus, Lawrence steadily peered at Emily while his body writhed and jerked against the restraints. She watched him with a stern face.

He had lied about cleaning his teeth before bed. How had mummy known? She stood behind him in the bathroom counting the minutes of his brushing. Each time he looked up into the basin mirror her immobile stare forced his head down.

Lawrence would not believe the red, soaked figure in the mirror was him. It was someone else. He looked straight into Emily's void irises, burned volcanic islands in their white ocean. He pleaded to the reflection.

Emily gave a gentle smile. He wanted to thank her. Thank you, mummy. He could rinse away the toothpaste. Emily moved the knife to the stocking securing his left wrist.

She sliced the flesh in two expert flicks.

'Don't beg,' she told the terrified face. 'You're a filthy girl. Little boys don't mess like that. Ugly, diseased, look at it.'

Lawrence felt his heart racing when it should be still, stupidly pumping the blood from his body. The morphine of physical weakness oozed through him, made him unable to muster thoughts. Each slid into some unrelated other things as he tried to hang on to one, playing catch as catch can in his head.

'This your wife?' Emily had pulled a photograph from the wallet inside his jacket. 'Nice dress. Suit me, that.'

His head was woozy. There was no pain, only rapid shivering over his entire body. Occasional lucid thoughts darted into his mind: she knew when the ticket inspector would pass, he must remember to buy the perfume, she had waited until the noisy track outside Crewe.

'No kids?' She had riffled through his wallet. 'Just a little woman waiting for her Lawrence to come home.' Emily jangled the fob of keys in the jacket pocket. 'Waiting for me.'

Lawrence heard a door click shut. He wondered what his wife had cooked for dinner. Somewhere a scratching sound as the lock was rolled to engaged. He remembered Emily hoping his wife had a pretty name. That was kind.

J.L. BROOKE

Lifesaving

He stared out at the bleakness of the winter canal basin. The roads along the ranks of narrow boats were stippled with cross breezes breaking between the warehouses. Above their roofs slate-shadowed clouds tumbled in from the west. Beyond their walls the brick-red waters raged down from the sandstone gorges. He shut his window on the distant roar.

Turning to the mirror he palmed off condensation. He had looked worse and felt better. It would be soon now.

At last he heard the car engine. The familiar sound, without comfort. A door banged in the alley. Another at the foot of the stairs. He jerked open his door as the boy's finger jabbed for the bell.

'I've told you not to point.'
'Dad!'
'It's rude.'
They wrestled into the kitchen.
'Coffee smells good!'
'Too good for you.'
'Where from?'
'Colombia.'

When he carried the mugs through, his son was lying on the carpet by the gas fire with an atlas open. As he set them down he saw a finger wander over southern Chile.

'Wrong end. Up a bit.'
He settled into his chair.
'In fact, up a lot.'
'It's not on this page!'
'Life's a bitch. Try turning it.'

When they went out to eat they took the path which skirted the basin to the river quay. They studied the cruisers among the narrow boats, choosing which they would take through the lock and onto the river. When the time came to go down to the sea.

On the headland above the cut a willow shivered, bowed, and straightened again. The flood was over the paving, coloured as the red stone itself. A step or two and into the spate, never to be found, creeled in the alder roots under the thicket banks.

The boy followed his gaze.

'You wouldn't live long in there, Dad.'

'Not so's you'd notice. How's the swimming?'

'Oh! I forgot. I got my bronze medallion!'

'Lifesaving?'

'Like you.'

'I took silver for survival first.'

'We don't do survival.'

'And the distance swimming?'

The boy's nose wrinkled.

'It's important, endurance.'

'Can I have chips instead of jacket?'

They had crossed the lock gate to the Old Trow and the chalked board by deserted benches. Smell of cooking gusted on the cold air. Inside, too, it was winter. Men huddled the bar, and women the log fire. In the bay window the boy claimed, the table shone unringed by glasses and the ashtray was polished clean. Out where the boats queued in summer the river swept by red and empty as a desert.

Here he had seen a rescue once. A woman fending off had leaned too hard on the boat hook and fallen between hull and quay. Then the current had swung the cruiser back in towards the wall. An old boatman had gone straight in. Leaving his beer. Feet first, surfacing with back to stone and boots against the boatside. Holding the gap until help came.

When they had him out he walked away. Heavy in wet clothes. Smiling at thanks from the crew and sarcastic humour from the benches.

He had followed the old man to the willow by the cut. There he fumbled something from a pocket, glanced to check, and chucked it underarm, as you would a sweet to a friend. Gleam of silver; small splash; a ring spreading downstream. As if a fish had leapt, no more.

Lifesaving

The boatman turned. 'She's a fair old river,' he said, without preamble. 'If ever you take what was hers, you just settle up.'

It was one of those stories at which his son had smiled politely, and which had not been told again. Yet it circled in his mind like an old log in an eddy, surfacing from time to time.

In the afternoon they played draughts. When his son pressed him hard he let him through to win. The boy made mugs of tea and placed them precisely, where the fire surround was broadest.

'I'm going to have a flat like this.'
'It's been all right. I'm tired of it now.'
'You going to move?'
'We'll see.'
'With Jenny?'
He placed the question like a cup.
'I'm not with Jenny any more.'
The boy took the information; fingered it gently.
'Oh.'
He grasped it more firmly, working the material. As his father had at the moment of being told, he felt the fullness of it: the happiness which would not be; the bleakness to remain.
'Right.'
He watched the boy set out the pieces again. More than careful now. Wind rattled the window, and rain spattered the panes.
'Soon be time,' he warned.
After the last game the boy cocked his head towards the alley.
'She's come.'
'I heard.'
'She's turning.'
He turned suddenly himself.
'I haven't packed my stuff.'
They worked quickly together, filling a plastic carrier in the kitchen with comics, chocolates, a new CD.
'Your pocket money.'
'Thanks, Dad.'
A horn sounded.
'She's waiting.'
'So I gather.'

The boy held out a hand to his father, who did not take it.
'See you next week, Dad.'
His face had the child's seriousness.
'Dad?'
'Yes?'
'See you then.'
He moved so that it was impossible to no longer shake hands.
'See you then, son.'
He listened until the familiar note of the engine had gone, and began to clear away.

Perhaps it had been the confusion over packing the carrier. When he brought the mugs into the kitchen he found the small silver coin on the table. Placed like a tip in a café.

Later, by lamplight, he walked to the willow. The water was higher now, and the distance less to its edge. Cold wind and narrow leaves brushed his face, but the coin was warm in his hand. He did not mark it, where it fell.

NICOLA WALDRON

School Rules

*Male staff,
when holding a child on their lap,
must use a cushion.*
Primary school notice board, South Wales

You have brushed past her silken shoulders
once too often and wonder
if the thrill of touching her
is more than your job's worth.

When she collects her register
from the narrow shelf,
you will find the occasion
to speak to her.
You will do it today.

You will not put the blonde child on your knee
when she comes looking for answers.
Her tears are not yours to wipe away.

You will tell her the solution lies
in the hard seat of her plastic chair,
in the fumbled tying of her shoelace.

When temptation stands trembling
at your side: be firm.
Use language as a pair of hands.

GEORGE HOBSON

Sun-Patch

Sun-patch quilted on the kitchen floor
By happy mediation of a window-pane:
It lies on mundane tiles, a semaphore,
Signaling an awesome, sweet refrain.

Noiselessly it slides across the tiles,
Swatch of tissue from the realm of Day;
Rides, bright sail, by scented isles
Of grapes and peaches on the lacquered tray.

Round the basket hanging from the beam,
Round the hempen ropes, it folds from day
To day, at the appointed hour, its pliant gleam,
Weightless, impalpable; and goes it way.

On the table, smoothed by centuries of hands,
It sets a comb of honey on the whorls;
Later, luminous on stone, the sun-patch stands
Trembling, alive to voices in the walls.

Now it bandages a broken chair, now stains
A chest; upon the objects in its path it plays,
For each in turn, a proper melody: strains
Otherwise unheard, of beauty and of praise.

To the kindling in the hearth it puts a flame; shines
Copper pot and ladle; streaks white
The blackened fire-back. Then suddenly the vines
Outside the window stir with wind, the light

Appears to shake, to flap its golden wings
As if to flee into the blue. Just seems:
The patch still sails beyond the shadow, sings
Still beyond our human being and our dreams.

Sun-Patch

See now: defying gravity, it gilds the stair
And bends around the wooden rail; unfurled
Again on stone, it melts away in air.

KEARAN WILLIAMS

The First Tourist Sends Out Two Thousand Questionnaires

We are not changing ground to escape from facts but rather to find them.
Louis MacNeice

I have recently despatched some letters of enquiry,
Together with my draughtsman and the boy of Mr Lloyd,
To a distant northern region in the hope of obtaining
A wholly accurate and exhaustive description
Of their castles, lakes and monuments, their picturesque views.

Sir, a troublesome knee prevents me leaving this parish,
But I pray you may afford these men your every hospitality.
Jameson is a draughtsman; please assist him with his maps
By marking each attraction for a gentleman of these shires.
My boy will have a sack for geological specimens,
There is much we wish to know of you; these papers are our inquest . . .

What is the frequency of beards among your people?
When they undress to wash, in what ways do they examine themselves?
Please give instances of your coachmen's typical shouts and gestures.
Is it true your hedgehogs suck at cattle's teats?

Jameson sends me missives, and I work at their translation.

The rocks of this region are dissoluble, black and shattery.
They sometimes weep a sweet-smelling butter good for rheumatism.

The women have glands which make them sob from their temples.
They spend the day in the saltmarshes shifting with the tide.

The air here is filled with the clamour of industry.
Boys study the Bible in a smoky, tar-stained shed.

We believe it a false charge concerning the hedgehogs,
Their mouths are too small, and the cows would not allow it . . .

The First Tourist Sends Out Two Thousand Questionnaires

My draughtsman returns, his notebook filled with head-shapes,
Tail peculiarities, a cartography of wrinkles.
The boy has brought me a sackful of peat
To inhale from every hearth and write, convinced
That what is in the soil is elsewhere on the surface,
(I have paced the shore, searching boulders for the Tropics,
Trained my spyglass for a glimpse of porpoise, plover, anything),
And find scored on each page a sad history of waves and bare feet
Freezing and gripping, the weather hurtling in.
All of it comes over. They are gathering in the halls
In their fine, old-weave tartan. Some of this may mean
Nothing to you, but my heart smoulders
Heavy as the peat – it's important and painful.
I would like to feel I belong in that country,
I sometimes think I was born there.

JOHN GURNEY

The Dying-Room

The Dying-Room's untidy. Feels unclean.
Paint's flaking from the window frames. Thick scores
from death-beds wound the walls, deface the scene
like signs of fights, memorials of wars.
Here being fights non-being. Now your eyes
reopen slowly, far less frequently.
They show deep irritation, real surprise
to find that you're still living. Patiently,
outside the door, the ventilation fan
is praying for another passing man.

No tube, of course. No drip to pierce your skin.
No current from a plastic bag of blood
to keep you in existence, ailing, thin,
and wasting with leukaemia. I am stood
beside you, sniffing roses. It is May.
A heavy scent of hawthorn swells the air,
that's tactile, like a pillow. Mothers play
with children in a garden. All despair
seems alien. Now the distant headland cliff
is glinting like a silver hieroglyph.

Its fulmars have returned. Two days ago
I watched them cross the wind in silent glides
on stiff thin wings, their breasts as white as snow
they'd battled in Alaska. Each would ride
the bluff's warm gusting updraught, tracked its edge
like figures in a ghost-dance. Now and then
their bodies dropped, would hurtle past a ledge,
then level out, and swiftly climb again
three hundred feet of whiteness. Soared with bliss
like soul-birds, in the heart of the abyss.

The Dying-Room

You reawaken, frightened. Overwrought,
you stare at me in terror, full of pain
as if you saw death's angel, read the thoughts
that gather round my body. You complain
your catheter is leaking. Now the nurse
is whispering I must leave you. You will cool
quite rapidly, she murmurs, as you curse
her fumblings at your bowels. The pack of stools
is gradually removed. I step outside.
Feel privy to an act of suicide.

FRANCES ANGELA

Strip-Wash

I'm standing half covered
in a vest in a round bowl
in the kitchen sink;
one hand reaching out
to steady myself
on the window-glass.

I can see the bottom
of the narrow stairs;
the clothes-line
pullied up to the ceiling
my father's overall straps
with the twinkling, silver buckles
hanging down.
And the top of my mother's dark head
as I struggle to balance
spreading my legs for her fingers
beneath the flannel.

WILLIAM SCAMMELL

Roots

Father called it a riphook, though
most people knew it as a sickle,
its steel blade curling in
a half-hug of air, inviting you
to shake hands with a little mayhem.

He swung and he swung, parting
the yellow stalks and powdery leaves
till his back creaked in pain.

Bill the ripper, mixed up with
lascivious brambles corkscrewed
into the hedge, man-eating thistles,
pagodas of weeds. Bill tasting
obedience to the love of a clammy T-shirt,
his tonsure of sweat, stalking about on
platform soles of mud, a blizzard of seeds
stuck fast in the ribs of his socks.

The roots reeled him in.
He sank closer and closer to the earth
and clung to his tools with his fists,
cross-hatched by stings and scratches.
Finally it was a matter of knees, hands,
fingers, pecking at the rich black carbons
with the mind, squatting there like a woman
about to give birth.

                    And the space
he had cleared looked back at him
an hour later, surprising them both
with its new arrangements, like a head
poked out of a long train on a curve.

JOHN DICK

Two Dreamings

You wouldn't have snakes in the house,
and even our quietest moments were immune
to dingo and cinnamon quail,

though somewhere on that street, a pregnant woman
swam in a sulphurous tide of flying ants,
and lightning spirits brushed the holly trees

at Gosden, where the Old Man lay awake,
fishing for catfish and dace
in a river of static.

So much of flesh was green, you found yourself
in ramsons and the taste of watercress,
in mullein and foxglove lighting the summer dusk

and yellow iris hanging in the porch
to keep us pure. You buried stones and feathers in a jar
to keep all thought of evil from the door,

while I constructed tunnels in the dark:
cockchafers; worms; a cobweb of blood on my tongue;
and all the time I longed for transformation,

hunting in the shadow of the house,
containing, like a spell, the magpie's call:
its cryptic love, its taste for carrion.

SHEENAGH PUGH

Sandman

Cloud has scrolled over again, and a cold wind
blows seals into the bay; black brows gleaming
on a gunmetal sea, and there is no-one left
on the beach except me and the naked man,

lying face down in the sand. He is growing paler
as he dries out: small silent grains are sliding
down the slopes of him, filling the hollow
of his back. Four sets of footprints lead away

from the body: his and his wife's, going straight ahead,
and a circling turmoil from the boy and girl,
too old for sandcastles, who took so much trouble
sculpting their murder victim. They were laughing

all the time, and the patient father, stretched out
on the beach to be posed and measured, was laughing too,
shaking his head, complaining his sepia likeness
was too short, building up muscles of sand . . .

His wife sat watching the dead man take shape
under her children's hands. She kept trailing
her fingers through her hair; as it fell back,
the grey would catch the light. She never laughed

with the others: even the brief smile flitting
across her face went out whenever she glanced
from her husband to the body like his.
When the sky darkened, and they were going,

she wanted to know if the tide would take him.
And they said no: he was above the mark,
and she left, reassured. I watched her out of sight
an hour since, and already his right hand has blurred

Sheenagh Pugh

into a white hummock. Wind shivers over him,
evening him out: soon the little sand-crabs,
scribbling their hasty messages on silence,
won't even have to pause when they come on him.

ALISON SPRITZLER-ROSE

Cows

This Wednesday the cows came home –
A herd the size of England, blanketing
the horizon with misshapen bumps, moving.
They came like exodus on a pit-stop:
Some only a few hours old,
Still wet on spindly legs,
Some still harnessed to ploughs,
Old ones with dusty udders
Swaying an inch from the ground.
They trampled Bramwell's farm
To a sodden pancake.

I had been dreaming a leopard
But the spots were larger, less close together.
I knew it wasn't a dream
When my nostrils woke to the ammonia sky –
The smelling salts of their administering.
Then the ohm mantra moo,
like a tuning fork – less heard than felt.

By daybreak the media had caught on.
Helicopters circled like angry border collies.
The airlift was a let down
And the journalists misunderstood.
The S.A.S. gave me tea with whisky.
Have I mentioned the fan mail?
I'm the envy of 800 million Indians!

They stayed three days, surrounding my house
And crowding the patches of August shade.
They fertilised and turned my land.
Now I'm growing prize orchids and giant yams.

STEPHEN DUNCAN

The Call-In

Broken yolk of dawn;
a squashed rabbit by the gate
has pink entrails
like a dish of cold food.

Only with my peppermints
can I face the lane
and pass on, sucking hard
this mouthful of peppery eggs

until the sweet shells break
with the shriek of rooks
and their black tumble
across the meadow.

I stretch my arms and throw
the psalm of my call-in,
sobbing from the back of my throat
the cries and bird-calls

until the white-patched shadows roll
and I can warble on
with the sibilants of sweets
a rude song of my own.

They know my full pockets,
tongues turning to rasp my arm
as I drive on the muddy rumps,
haloes of steam rising from their backs.

And when they disobey
on the long mile-walk down,
trotting past the milking shed
and grumpy Da for the river,

The Call-In

water draughts pulsing like snakes
through their necks,
I suck hard and leap in,
calling for them all again:

for the cat who picks at pink icing,
for my horse munching stale Xmas cake,
for the old cow's head at the window
scraping jam jars clean,
her long wet ham of a tongue
rolling deep inside the glass.

ADAM SCHWARTZMAN

Under the Blue-Printed Sky

Under the blue-printed sky or in hotel rooms
the smart young aides slept,
who were none the poorer when the crinkled rills
began turning back up the creeks,
and the wavy streams repaired to the hills.
For a time the air was still
a nice colour for a shirt,
the flowers still crazy with light.

Their leaving was nothing more
than a hair lifting, than the turning of the wind,
a brushing against a cheek,
though eventually everyone began dreaming
of rain, became haunted by the ammonia smell
of the long-overdue afternoon squalls
whipping by in profile,
and sooner or later, rocked

in the *primum mobile* of their huddled sleep,
it would be them in the city-bound carriages,
imagining the sound of the train
become the sound of storms,
while up the sun drove into the sky
in perennial white and slowly
the land lost its memory for knowing
who, where, why, how many, how many times before.

TANYA WINTER

Gone Fishing

Silently, in the soft evening sunshine,
she sits sewing; her needle glinting
as she deftly darts it
through the pale green fabric.
Down it dives, dragging the thread,
like the line cast by a fisherman
hurling his bobbin out to sea.

Swiftly, her needle swims
through the crests of the waves
she makes; pale green of puckering fabric,
swallowing each stroke
which breaks the surface.

Late evening draws on;
the setting sun hauled in,
advancing night spreads its net.
Her dress finished,
she slips it on
and rows out
to catch her man.

PHIL BOWEN

Frank's Old Mansion

Where the action was always available for the big boys in pieces, though they
all had their various stabs at being head of the home; Frank's method – one
over the arm of the chaise – would be to count every berry on the wallpaper
then he'd say: and that just about sums this household up.

When each afternoon seemed spent at 'Joker's': the cops and the snouts
in it together mooching through the smoke, conniving something out of
what a little bird had said – Joker in that famous bowler – a crooked cross
against his Nellie's life, dancing attendance on the Plain Clothes,

whose eyes would flit beneath trilbies like characters out of a cast in order
of appearance, a clue then an itch of shail inside the barmaid's slingback;
a thrupenny bit on the edge of the baize, the note left beside Press Button B
for the conman running away to somewhere else to run away to

where the light's always on but there's nobody in now at Frank's old mansion;
the phone off at the Rialto ballroom, stroke cinema, stroke second-hand settees
where kids on the 73 played spot-the-whiteman before they smashed it flat in '
Out of Africa, Joker said he thought 10.30. meant opening not closing time,

his mouth full of chicken, he'd bet on the next fly, get whatever it was
you wanted, his girls canoodling with the C.I.D. a laced drink for each whaler
under Orion's belt, and Joker, taking care of business, damp bank notes
stacked in his old Zephyr's boot. Then that time Mervyn hurtled straight through

the traffic lights, hit the bus stop, shot right over the roundabout,
telling the young bobby now he'd flown Spitfires, Hurricanes, for the puny likes
of him at least ten times more pissed than this. Then Hugh with his Jags:
sixteen suits and you couldn't tell the new one; how he got off the Irish boat

back in the late forties, the only things with him, two shirts and a verb.
It doesn't matter which. Time to see Nancy. Table service. Ice in all
the water jugs – a fondness for those little dogs – trays of Black and Whites,
Monty the barrister the only one adamant that his had to be Vat.

Frank's Old Mansion

nk! Mervyn closed a deal once on Nancy's apron. Spend! He'd think nothing
lying to the Isle of Man for a packet of Passing Cloud. And supposing
as Vat in all the bottles. So? Nancy's entitled to her little perks.
gh! We're not a restaurant, you'd get told if anyone dare ask her for crisps.
l behind every window where Hire Purchase has been agreed,
h lodger who kept an expectant woman awake, the one stood whistling
the conman running away to somewhere else to run away to
re the light's always on but there's nobody in now at Frank's old mansion.

BRIAN MCMANUS

Songs of Praise

(Lockerbie Parish Church, December 1988)

They came to sing their songs and praise his name,
And took their seats in rows of polished yew;
But nothing in their lives would be the same.

Outside, the clouds replete with salty rain,
The restless heavens waiting for their cue;
They came to sing their songs and praise his name.

The preacher rolls the dice to start the game,
As plates of burnished silver claim their due;
But nothing in their lives would be the same.

The stars resigned to hang their heads in shame,
Unable to prevent their passing through;
They came to sing their songs and praise his name.

The preacher stokes the fire, fans the flame,
Replenishes, recharges faith anew;
But nothing in their lives would be the same.

The heavens and the stars were not to blame.
Seek, and ye shall find the one who knew;
They came to sing their songs and praise his name,
But nothing in their lives would ever be the same.

SYLVIA OLDROYD

Earth-Stars

In spaces between beeches they appear
at the season of firefall, unobtrusive
knobs of brown among past years' litter,
showers of small meteorites.

As each ripens, its outer wall curves back
below the speed of sight, to form
the outline of a star; now we notice them,
exclaim with pleasure at familiar shapes

more star-like than their namesakes.
Inside, the sporangium waits
through an aeon of plant-time, for a finger
of wind, the vibration of a rain-drop

to quicken a supernova; spores puff out,
nebulous, purple-brown smoke
carried on lifting airs to populate
spaces between beeches with a new star-rise.

JO PESTEL

Casualty

I'm absent today Miss

Yesterday
The high geese strained
Blue-flying homewards to new nesting

I have a note from my parents, Miss.
It will explain.

Now over there, the yellow dustbin sits squat
With softening outlines
And unhesitating receptionists clip across spaces
Now in the chair next to mine
A blurring lady babbles quietly.
'I've been married for thirty-nine years you know
Never once had an argument.'
She worries about her cash card.

I'm not sure when I'll be back, Miss.
What lessons have you done?

Now I see an undulating down pipe.
Remembersee it straight
Hunchbacked faces leer and the edges of the world
Ripple along me.
Cashcard got on well with her colleagues but
Never had a special friend.
'Never in all that time. Strange, isn't it?'

The nurse is impatient.
'How much of the card can you see?'
How can I know what I do not see?
Remembersee? Insee?

Casualty

Will I be able to catch up Miss?
Will you tell me what to do?

Now is
A camellia called Anticipation
Softperfect petals pink in candlelight
Real presence. Holy holy holy
Bow down.

SARAH CARR

The Open Mouth

In the quiet collision
of odours in the daytime,
and the whistling reek
in the night,
she smelled like
apricots swelling.

She sat slowly,
tenderly vibrating
in the silence,
feet tied and
hands ill at ease
at her tied feet.
Gilded like peace
and like sighing.

We came towards her,
as simple as glass.
Our petitions under
microscopes seemed like
laws of the land.

In winter mirrors
our heads were like
ashen blocks
and we have sat in
tubs of grace,
the warmth of which
stung our eyes.
We lost our fingernails
in books and stole
bags of beads and clots.

The Open Mouth

With our skin as tight
as a bird's
we stood before her.
She made the noise
of a quiet birthing animal.
We looked into her mouth
and it was full of light.

DAVID ALMOND

The Time Machine

Felling Shore, early May, the year before my father dies. The first time I've nested in years. I'm in ancient hawthorn, with a hedgesparrow's egg in my mouth. From outside comes birdsong, the endless din of the distant city, then a grinding of gears and engines, the crunch of wheels on damaged roads. I step higher onto a thin bough, pull aside the tangles of foliage. I see caravans and lorries coming down through the terraced streets, mounting the broken kerbs on to the waste ground, entering this broad field above the Tyne. The tree that holds me quivers as I grip it tighter. Its thorns pierce my skin. I see The Waltzer and The House of Death. A sheep, a goat and a little camel lie in the same cage. I slip, the egg bursts on my tongue. I gag and spit. Salt and slime in my mouth. The shell ineffably fine. The ruined egg dangles from my lips. I grip a new branch, re-balance, stare out again. Through the hawthorn blossom I see the Time Machine return to Felling Shore.

I climb down, squat in the shade of the tree. The convoy comes to rest. Children and dogs leap from its doors to the field. I spit and spit, wipe my mouth with my sleeve. Blood trickles from my hands. A group of the children come. A little girl in a short frock with an alsatian at her side points at me, then at the old shoe box at my side.

What's in there? she says.

I open the box, show the eggs laid in neat rows on smooth sand. I touch them with my fingers, name them.

Starling, larky, blackbird, wren.

I point up into the tree, to the nest deep in the foliage.

Hedgesparrow, I tell her.

I pick a fragment of shell from the tip of my tongue.

Give us an egg, she says.

I hold out the bright blue fragment to her.

She laughs, grips the growling dog by its mane. Beyond her,

The Time Machine

men are already uncoupling trailers, throwing rods and girders down onto the grass, unrolling great sheets of canvas. I see the exposed facade of The Time Machine, sky blue, with pyramids and flying saucers and fleshy pink women in bathing costumes painted on it, at the centre the arched entrance with its beaded curtain.

A skinny naked boy crouches before the eggs, shoves his finger into the sand. I clip his hand away.

Which one you from? I ask the girl.

We tell your age for sixpence. Dad gets out of chains and sticks skewers in himself. Mam tells your fortune and shows her tits to men after midnight. She held her hand out. Give us a penny, eh?

What's your name?

Little Kitten. She shows her nails like claws. You're fourteen. Give us a penny.

I drop a coin in her palm and she giggles and spits then sets off to the river with the dog and her friends. Out in the field, older children are roaming now. A juggler spins knives. Elvis singing Hound Dog begins to crackle and roar. I move out from the tree. The woman leaning against the Time Machine hails me as I walk by. She is blonde, plump like the women in the paintings. I see how the name and the bodies have been painted time and again.

Yes you, boy, she calls.

She wears high heels, short skirt. Make-up is caked on her face, her eyes are rimmed by black mascara. I begin to turn away, then catch my breath at the tenderness I see in her. She is thirty, or older, or even my mother's age. She smiles, she licks her lips, she tugs gently at the straps beneath her white blouse. I stare at the entrance to the Time Machine, at the darkness inside.

Make sure you come and see the Time Machine, she says.

I stare at her.

Remember, she whispers. Remember, bonny boy.

I turn my eyes away, I leave the field, I hurry home.

Dust seethes in the sunlight that pours into the kitchen. Light flares in the loose strands of my sisters' hair. We gaze at the eggs. We practise naming them, remembering them.

Blackbird, we whisper. Starling, larky, wren.

David Almond

I show them the paired pinholes in each egg, tell them how to blow out the stuff from inside. I tell them it was Dad who taught me all this, who years ago took Colin and me through the old lanes at Felling's edges. The rules he'd taught me: silence and speed, no damage to any nest, only one egg and then only when the clutch was three or more.

I see tears in Catherine's eyes.

What's wrong? I said. What's wrong?

She raises her hand into the streaming light. We watch the dust in silvery fragments dance and seethe about us.

Human skin, she says. They told us at school – the majority of dust is human skin. Dead skin.

We meditate upon this. We laugh. The dust rises and falls, we watch it stream into our mouths with breath.

Angels are like this, says Catherine. Their bodies are subtler than ours. Their atoms are dispersed. They are more spirit than matter. They are all around us.

We look at her.

They told us at school, she says. It's true.

We all laugh again.

It's true, says Mary and Margaret together. It's very true.

It is, I say. And I saw a Time Machine today.

Dad comes in from the sunlight. He has his heavy herringbone coat over his arm. He kisses the girls and sits with us and sighs at the beauty of the day. He lights a Player's and the smoke weaves and spirals through the dust. He shifts on the hard kitchen chair, catches his breath.

Press there, he says, taking my hand, holding it against the base of his spine. I press, feel the complicated solid bone beneath the flesh and skin.

There? I ask.

There. Yes, there, Press harder, son.

He touches the eggs gently and tells us he had seen a Time Machine today.

I know, I say. I saw it come to Felling Shore.

He breathes the smoke from his nostrils.

I saw it going down, he says. Just as it did those years ago.

He reaches out and touches my cheek.
Who'd believe it? Just as it did when I was your age, all those years ago.
We lean close together, above the eggs.
You'll have to take me, he says. Won't stay long. You'll have to show me.
He laughs, touches us all, kisses us all.
He ponders.
Larky? he said. Blackbird, starling and wren?

I dream that God clambers through the hawthorn at Felling Shore. He balances on thin boughs, gazes into the nests, carefully takes eggs from clutches of more than three. He holds them on His tongue for a moment then swallows them. Little Kitten watches Him from the ground. She keeps saying, Give us an egg, sir. Please give us an egg. At last He tosses one down to her. It cracks open on her palm as she catches it. A feathered child comes out, tiny as a damsel fly. I catch my breath. It is our dead sister, Barbara, the fourth of us. I watch her fluttering towards the blue sky and deserts of the Time Machine. Forgive us, whispers Little Kitten. Give us another egg, sir. But God is furious. He glares darkly down at the girl. He becomes careless and clumsy. He shoves egg after egg into His mouth. Yellow yolk and bright blue shell dribble from His lips. The hedges tremble and the air is filled with the alarm cries of parent birds. I see Barbara flutter through the beaded curtain of the Time Machine. I rush to follow her, wake in the darkness inside.

Next afternoon Dad calls me from the garden. He is tying the stems of roses against the fence. He squeezes a bud and we see the petals packed moist and dense inside. He tells me how fortunate I am. He tells me there will be nothing I can't do.
You understand, don't you? he says.
I nod.
He smiles, ironic, blows smoke on the aphids to make them die.
We'll go now, he says. Just you and me, the two of us. I'll take the others later.

David Almond

In the house the girls and Mam are at the kitchen table. Colin is somewhere upstairs, trying on his best yellow shirt or his best blue jeans.

He takes me inside, brushes my hair down, tugs at my sleeves and hems to make me neat. He lays his herringbone coat across his arm. He sighs, presses his hand into the small of his back.

Where are you two off to? says Mam.

He grins and winks. Nesting, he says. He kisses the girls. I'll take you to the fair later, he says. I won't forget.

We step out into the streaming light.

Goodbye, little chicks, he calls.

An untidy cluster of tents and stalls, a couple of roundabouts turning. The caravans are parked above the water. The din of compressors, Elvis' howl, the scent of onions and boiling fat. The people of Felling move at ease through the field and through the fair. We pause by the hawthorn at the edge of the field. Brilliant light pours down, carries the singing of larks from somewhere high above. Dad faces me, watches me. I see the darkness of his beard beneath his dark skin, the heavy eyebrows, the glittering eyes. I see that soon I will be taller than him.

Are you happy? he asks.

I shade my eyes and look away.

Not fair, he says. He raises his hand to some passers-by. You will be happy. You will have everything we've missed.

We move forward. He lights a Player's. We weave our way through the crowds between the shooting galleries and roundabouts. I feel his hand guiding me forward. Little Kitten stands in the walkway wearing a white dress calling out that she can tell the age of anyone for sixpence. She catches my arm as we pass. She points to Dad. Forty two, she tells him. She holds out her hand. Give us me sixpence, then. He laughs and tosses the coin to her.

She winks at me.

Give us an egg, she squeaks.

We move on.

It's unimaginable, he says. It's the same Time Machine as in my day. The same woman, the same man. They can't be.

The Time Machine

The woman stands on a low stage before the facade. She wears net tights, a bathing costume whose stiff bodice shimmers like a kingfisher's wing. There is an older man beside her, in black top hat and tails. The beaded curtain is pulled back to expose a cool blue interior. The man leans out towards the gathering crowd. He scans our faces.

Who is bold enough to enter the Time Machine? he calls.

The woman smiles, so gentle.

Who could cope with the journey? she asks. Who could understand what will be seen?

I gaze up at her. Dad's hand rests in the small of my back, impelling me. She catches my eye, her gaze moves on.

The man holds a glittering black rock to us.

He tells us. Here is a stone brought back from the Moon.

He holds a curved piece of brass.

The breastplate of a Centurion, he calls.

He shows a framed indecipherable script.

A writing from the ninth millennium, he whispers.

He leans closer.

What will the next voyager bring back? What wonder will be added to our marvellous museum?

She catches my eye again. She leans to me.

Who will travel with Corinna in the Time Machine?

There is laughter in the crowd. Some kid calling, Me! Me! Dad's hand stretches across my back. You, he whispers. You!

Corinna grins, leans down again.

You? she asks. This bonny boy?

And reaches down for me, I find my hand in her own, find myself stepping upward, hear Dad behind me laughing and calling: Remember me!

They hold me between them on the stage. The man grips my shoulders, runs his hands over my arms and hips. Call me Morlock, he tells me. Her peers deep into my eyes. He asks my name, my school and I answer softly while Corinna holds my hand and tells me to be brave.

Are you intelligent? he asks. Can you remember what has been shown to you?

I nod. Yes. My head is reeling. I hear laughter and mockery from the crowd. I see the open curtain of the Time Machine.
What are your ambitions? says Morlock.
I gulp, reel.
To be happy, I say.
Happy! Then what are your dreams? he says. What are your visions? What wonders have come in your young life?
I stare down at Dad. His eyes burn, they urge me to reply.
Corinna strokes my cheek.
Be brave, she whispers.
I see Little Kitten laughing at me from between the stalls. A huge man bound in heavy chains lumbers through the field outside.
What are your dreams? says Morlock.
I see God, I whisper. I see babies flying. I go to Heaven and Hell. I see the dead come back to life.
Morlock laughs. He slaps my back, shakes my hand.
We have chosen well, Corinna. Take him inside and make the preparations.
She turns me towards the entrance.
Who else will come inside? calls Morlock. Who will see our voyager set off on his journey through the ages? Who will enter our marvellous museum and learn of the intrepid voyagers from the past. Who will be there when the boy returns with his stories and his souvenirs . . .?
We enter the blue interior, and behind us the people of Felling begin to step up to pay and follow . . .

Inside: a translucent canopy, straw spread upon the grass, shelves bearing caskets and cupboards, another low stage, the machine itself. An upright cylinder, tall and broad as a hawthorn tree, made of timber, heavily-varnished. Lights fixed in vertical rows, purple and red, clocking as they flash on and off, on and off. A large dial like a barometer, The Past to the left, the Future to the right. A door with heavy brass fittings. In flaking golden paint upon the curved surface, its name: The Time Machine.
I imagine that disintegration will be necessary for time travel,

that I will be broken up in there, that my atoms will be dispersed, my being abstracted in order that I can slip subtly through the great solids of space and time. Perhaps I tremble at this. Corinna puts her arm around my shoulder. I smell her perfume and her sweat, feel how harsh the fibre of her bodice is, the hardness of the bones that keep it in place, then above this the soft flesh of her shoulders and breasts. She cups my chin in her palm, kisses me gently on the cheek, asks me to say my name.

We choose our travellers for their looks and their brains and the wanderlust we see in their eyes, she whispers. I'll be with you. I'll tell you what you must do and what you must say.

She kisses me again.

Everything will be fine. Wherever we take you, it will be fine.

She presses her finger to my lips as Morlock leads the audience in.

They gather before us, they grin. Dad laughs from the back of the crowd. Morlock stands beside me again, tells the crowd he can feel the strength in me.

The future or the past? he asks me.

I catch Dad's eye again.

The future, I say.

He pulls a lever in the stage and the machine begins turning, rattling and rumbling gently on castors set into the stage. The lights flash more urgently. He hauls the lever back and slowly the machine ceases its turning. He stares into my eyes. He says that he can feel my readiness for astounding flight. He presses a button beside the dial.

Take him in, Corinna, he says. Lead him to the future.

She leads me to the threshold.

Morlock shakes my hand, kisses Corinna, turns to the crowd again.

While this boy travels through the ages, I will take you on a tour of our museum. Take him in, Corinna.

She opens the door, guides me inside. I look back to see the crowd gazing intently after us, Dad waving. The door slides shut, the outer wall begins to turn. Corinna giggles.

In here, she says, opening another door, pushing me gently in.

David Almond

A small square room, a still and peaceful place. Yellow padding on the walls, a padded bench, a shelf of books. Names and dates scratched and carved in the timber door and on the timber between the padding. Blue light filters down through frosted glass in the ceiling. We sit side by side on the bench. Our thighs touch each other's, our outstretched feet touch the opposite walls. I brace myself, hear the rumbling of the outer shell as it plunges through the ages.

When we return, says Corinna, Mr Morlock and the crowd will ask you some questions. You'll want to know the answers, won't you?

She reaches up to the shelf above our heads and brings down a folder with *The Shape Of Things To Come* inscribed on its cover. She spreads it over our linked knees, begins to turn its pages. Inside are photographs and drawings and film stills. There are rockets and flying saucers and groups of gentle citizens strolling beneath trees. I see how Corinna's nails are bitten to the quick. The flesh of her thighs swells at each of the thousand holes in her fishnet tights. She puts her arm around me, she speaks to me gently.

You must say that we found ourselves in a great city. There were buildings all around us that touched the sky. The people wore silken robes and travelled in tiny flying machines. You must say that in the future we will travel to the stars in the blinking of an eye. Machines will do our chores. Disease will be conquered. The savagery of our natures will be tamed and there will be no war. We will begin to communicate telepathically. We will begin to understand how we may make true contact with the dead. All of us will travel easily through time.

She cups my chin in her palm.

Yes, she says. We chose well. Listen. This is also what you must say.

I gaze into her eyes. I listen, and am disappointed by these bland and unsurprising visions. I think of Dad outside. I think of my sister mingling with the earth. I think of dust and angels and of the salty slime that can become a flying thing. I feel her leg against my leg. I turn my eyes from her. I seek the image of a damsel fly, and read the names carved into the machine's heavy timber. They form an intricate deep pattern of letters and numbers. The most recently carved are readable. Those beneath are losing definition. Those from the distant past have many times been written over. Obscured, they exist as clues, fragments, meaningless cuts in the grain.

Corinna touches my cheek.

Yes, she tells me. You can add your name.

With the tip of the knife she gives me I inscribe myself alongside these unknown others. I name myself, I name the place in which I name myself, I name the year in which I name myself. I finger the lettering, trace the outlines of my oblivion.

Corinna draws me to her once more.

This is yours, she says.

There is money in her palm. She draws me closer. She kisses me on the lips. She presses the coins into my palm. Yes, this is yours. I know you'll answer well, so this is yours.

She touches my cheek, my lips.

Keep our secret and you can come to visit me at night.

She smiles. My face rests on her shoulder, I look into the shadow between her breasts.

It's true, she whispers. You can come to see me. She laughs. Would you like that?

I nod. I bite my lips. I inhale her perfume, her sweat. I hear her heart beating as the Time Machine rumbles on.

Everything will be fine, she whispers. Keep our secret, answer the questions. Let me test you. Where did we go to? What did we see?

I answer well. She grins and applauds.

What will be defeated? she whispers.

Death, I say.

I lie there for an age with my cheek upon her breast. She whispers that I am a brave one, a perfect time traveller. I almost sleep. I begin to dream of my father breaking into fragments, travelling to the future alongside me. Then Corinna shows me a little glass jar, filled with earth. I lift the lid, rub the earth between my fingers, feel the dry grit, the fine dust, nothing growing there.

Our little souvenir, she says. Earth from the far future.

Soon the Time Machine begins to slow, returning us to Felling Shore, early May, the year before my father dies . . .

Dad laughs as we stand there, Corinna and Morlock and I, before the little crowd beneath the blue canopy. We show the jar of earth, we allow the spectators to dip their fingers into it. My head reels at the questions that are called to us. With Morlock's and Corinna's help, I answer. We came to a great city. There was work for everyone, though many days were spent in leisure. The planets seemed as close as countries do now. We understood the nature of God and we saw how his spirit shines in everything. Yes, each of us will be able to travel through time. Yes, we will indeed be happier then. At last, Morlock puts his arm around me. He says the boy is exhausted. He announces that it is over. He tells the crowd that they have seen a wondrous thing and that they may go now. They leave, whispering, wondering, laughing. Dad waits and we step down from the stage.

I travelled in the Time Machine as a boy, he says.

Morlock smiles.

Ah! In my father's day. In Corinna's mother's day.

Corinna kisses me. She whispers, Don't forget, Make sure you come to me.

Morlock carries the earth to the museum. Corinna waits for us to leave.

We go out and the day is already darkening.

Outside another tent, a woman has many veils draped upon her. She holds open a curtain to inner darkness, a sign above her promises Salome's legendary dance.

Little Kitten squeals at us: Forty two! Forty two!

Dad asks, Did you see my name in there?

I search my memory, attempt to see again the great confusion of names and places and dates.

He laughs, nudges me, breathes smoke into the air.

It was in there, that's the main thing, even if it's unreadable now.

I see many watching me, the boy who travelled in the Time Machine.

Outside, there is the man wrapped in chains with a hatful of money before him on the grass. He struggles and squirms before his little crowd.

Beneath the hawthorn we look up towards the cheeping chicks and I recall the shape of God.
Dad watches me and grins as we walk on.
You enjoyed that, then?
He laughs.
Keep the secret, eh? don't forget.

Next morning Dad takes the girls to Felling Shore. I linger at home. I rearrange the eggs in my shoeboxes. I open the boxes of eggs that Dad has kept since his own youth. I match the eggs of the past with the eggs of the present: starling with starling, blackbird with blackbird, larky with larky, wren with wren. I can find no differences between them. My mother watches me and asks about my sadness. The light pours down upon us. I want to ask her about the loss of one who was formed in her own body. I want to ask her about the absences and angels that are all around us. I want to ask her why eggs are taken from clutches of more than three.
We gaze at each other through the brilliant seething dust. She touches my cheek and smiles. We do not know that this is the year before my father dies.
They return mid-afternoon. They laugh about The House of Death with its ghosts and bats, the little camel that they rode across the shore on. They shudder at the man who pushed skewers through his cheeks. They say that Little Kitten knows the ages of us all. We nibble coconut flesh and sip its milk. Colin sits with us in his yellow shirt. He tells us that last night he rode The Waltzer far into the dark. He taps a fast rhythm on the table, recalling a frantic song.
Later I lie in the garden, in the glare. Dad works at the trellis and the borders and keeps watching me. Blackbirds fly into the hedges with food. I finger the dry soil, dream of a whole world slowly becoming dust, shudder as the day begins to close.
At dusk I am by the garden gate. I want to be carried through time, back into the hawthorn tree, back to the first ever time I nested. I want to be carried to the distant nest when the dying is done and we all are re-assembled. Dad stands beside me. His hand is at the small of my back, pressing me gently forward. He smiles as

he sends me out on the errand that he knows is necessary but will be in vain. I move down through the gathering dark. I hear the distant grinding of gears and engines. By the time I gain the shore I know that the convoy has travelled on, that Morlock, Corinna and the Time Machine have gone. I stand beneath the hawthorn. I see other figures at the fringes of the field, understand that I am just one of several disappointed shades gathered on Felling Shore this night.

RON SMITH

The Last Time We Talked

Larry sits across from me at lunch and I know he's thinking much the same as I am. What the hell's happened to this guy over the last sixteen years?

He takes a sip from his water and then watches the ice cubes swirl around the glass. I'm taking in my usual overdose of caffeine, spiked with too much sugar and cream. At least I've quit smoking.

He's asking himself the obvious things: Do I look as bad as he does? Do I look as old? I know I haven't lost as much hair or put on as much weight. The guy's a lard ass. And his wife, what about his wife? She was attractive back then. What's she look like now? Could she possibly look as tired, as worn down as he does? He's asking himself about my wife, my Annie, which kind of pisses me off.

I look at my hands. No callouses. My hands are soft and pink, fleshy, and my life line forks in the middle of my palm. I used to move around the squash court like a tomcat. Now I can't roll off my couch without feeling winded. I admit it, I'm in rotten shape.

There's nothing subtle about the way we look at each other. Sixteen years will do that to your perspective. I look, but I don't see. This is not someone I know, not quite. I watch him closely. I want to see more than some physical similarities to the memory I'm dredging up. Hell, I have enough trouble with the picture I see of myself when I look at the wedding photograph Annie keeps on the mantlepiece.

But Larry and I had been good friends. When we went for a beer after an hour of squash, we always had something to say to each other. Small talk mostly, about sports or music. Occasionally, when one of us needed help, we'd confide in the other.

As I say, we were friends. I figure that history will help get us over this initial shock.

How's Carla, I ask.

He sucks in some air, looks me straight in the eye and says

nothing. He drops his gaze to the menu and recites the entrees, as if I'm retarded.

I had talked to Carla two nights earlier, shortly after I'd arrived at the Centre. I checked in, got the schedule for meals and sessions, and then the lecture on curfew and booze from a short, stout woman who made it clear I wasn't going to jerk her around. Her eyes were huge. All the rules were for my benefit, she pointed out.

I agreed. I assumed this would show I was going to be cooperative. Receptive to the therapy.

After I'd unpacked my gear, I sprawled out on one of the three narrow beds in the room. I studied the ceiling and thought, this is not going to be easy. This is prison. With day passes handed out at the discretion of the warden I'd just met. And worst of all, I'd volunteered myself for this experiment. So far I was lucky, no one had showed up to share my room. Or toilet and shower. This would be a bonus, to be on my own. When I broke into the sweats, I could deal with my demons alone. The idea of sharing my paranoia with someone else made me feel unclean. Besides, I figured if I could stand two weeks of looking at the photo wallboard someone had used to decorate the room, I'd probably survive the cure.

Everyone had insisted I try therapy. Group therapy, for Christ's sake. I don't much like talking about myself, at least not about the intimate stuff. And especially not to a bunch of strangers. Still, I knew as well as anyone else that I needed to get my life back on track. The last two flashes of temper had scared the shit out of me. Smashing crockery was one thing, but when you started to grab family around the neck, well, crazy came to mind. That's what hurt. The striking out. Wondering if I might bust someone's head open.

The ceiling was made up of two hundred and sixteen, one foot by one foot tiles. I tried to calculate the dimensions of the room but I'd never been much good at maths. Then I lay perfectly still and listened to my breathing. As my chest rose and fell, I thought about phoning Larry and Carla. I tried to understand the connection between my counting, my breathing, and them, but I couldn't see one. What a waste of time, I decided. The mind just works that way sometimes.

Larry and Carla had moved from the city up to this small town on the Sunshine Coast about a year after Annie and I moved to Vancouver Island. Larry had landed some work on a new television series. Before that he had done some freelancing on major films. But the work was intermittent and this series promised something more steady. The script called for a small seaside town with an active harbour. Larry discovered Gibsons. At least the producers credited him with the discovery. And that was enough to guarantee him employment for as long as the show ran.

Just before we left, Carla had become seriously ill. After a couple of weeks of tests, no one seemed able to diagnose her problem. The doctors advised hospitalization. Still no one knew what was wrong with her. We could see the lesions developing up and down her arms and legs but no one could stop them. The wounds spread and grew. They turned dark brown and then black. They looked like craters in her skin. She had been so beautiful, Annie said. Specialists were flown in from the Mayo Clinic and some place in Florida. Nothing changed. We visited her a few times in hospital, but the sight of her turned my stomach. Annie's too. Once we'd settled on the Island, the separation grew into silence. Neither Annie nor I had the words.

Later we heard Carla had been released from St. Paul's and they had moved. Here. When I suggested to Annie that I might look them up, she had said, Are you sure? Do you think you should? After all this time? Christ, Axel, she might have died! It's been sixteen years! What will you say to Lar if she's dead?

Sorry? I had asked, a little too sarcastically.

Annie had made a fist.

I'll tell him I'm sorry. What else would you have me say?

Annie had been right. Getting up the nerve to make the phone call had been harder than I thought it would be.

I climbed off the bed, put on a clean shirt and made my way to the office. Three men and a woman sat in the large stuffed chairs in the common area on to which all the rooms faced. The woman said something about taking chances but the context was lost on me. One of the men smiled in my direction as I walked by, but all I could think about was the phone call. The warden sat behind her desk. She looked downright unfriendly. Her hair was grey and knotted up in a bun at the back.

I rapped lightly on the doorjamb and said, Excuse me. Have you got a phone?

We both stared at the phone on her desk.

There are pay phones in the entrance, she said. All clients are required to use the pay phones.

I turned and looked down the hall. I could see the phones in their little cubicles but no phone books.

Sorry to bother you again, I said, but I don't have the number.

She squeezed her lips tight, reached into a drawer and placed a phone book on her desk. Her chubby hand rested on the cover. These have a way of walking out of here, she said. So it doesn't leave the room. Understand?

I nodded. Charmer, I wanted to say.

I had stewed over the thought of making this phone call for a couple of weeks. Now I had to fight to get the number. I flipped through the pages to the M's. I half expected not to find the name. But there it was. L.J. McCormack. And the number. Perhaps it was a coincidence. I had never known Larry's middle initial. This could be somebody else altogether. The name's not that uncommon, I thought.

The warden placed a pen and pad of paper in front of me. I wanted to tell this sweetheart to mind her own business. I wanted to tell her that making off with a phone book was not exactly my idea of big-time crime. Instead I wrote down the number.

Thanks, I said, and pushed the book towards her.

Good luck, she said.

I looked at her and grinned. How did she know? For a few moments I thought she could see right through me. I hated that. She could see my fear. I didn't like that. What if Carla was dead?

As I walked down the hall I wondered what the hell I was afraid of. I always feel uneasy about making a phone call and getting the wrong party. Sure I know I can hang up and no one will be any

The Last Time We Talked

the wiser. Yet when I hear a voice at the other end of the line that I don't know, I always get flustered and blurt out some silly apology, as if I've busted in on a couple making love. As if I've committed a crime. I know I've made the call. That's the point. And no matter what I do, no matter how I explain it to myself, or what I say to the person at the other end, if I dial a wrong number, I feel like I've made a damned fool out of myself. Annie says that that's stupid. No one will remember, even if they know.

But I would, I say. I'd remember.

The phone had rung eight times.

Hello.

A woman answered.

Her voice paralyzed me. I wanted to hang up. I'd hoped Larry would answer. Chances were I'd recognize his voice. I couldn't remember what Carla's voice sounded like. Whoever the woman was she sounded tired. I'd probably wakened her.

Hello, she said again.

Is this the McCormack place? I asked.

I felt stupid. What did I expect? I'd just looked up the number. But was it the right McCormack? And was this Carla?

I mean, I said, is this the L.J. McCormack who works in film and television?

Did, the voice said. Used to. Doesn't anymore.

The line went quiet. And then the voice spoke, the mouth a little closer to the phone.

Who is this, anyway?

Carla had always been feisty. This was a good sign.

Axel Sterne, I said.

Axel? I could hear her hesitate before she said, Axel, you asshole, it's ten thirty at night!

Carla?

Who were you expecting?

I don't know, I said. I don't know who I expected.

How was I supposed to tell her what I was thinking? I couldn't just say, So you're alive, are you? Annie and I thought you might be dead. My free hand waved in the air as if I were batting away each silly thought that popped into my head.

What? she said.

Well, you know how it is these days? With marriage and all?

You and Annie still together? she asked.

Yes, I answered.

Who would have thought, I heard her say. Jesus, Axel, we must be the only ones on the bloody planet who are still on our first marriages. She laughed. And it ain't from want of trying to leave, she said. God knows, Right?

I wondered what she meant. Was she referring to her illness? Or had she heard something about Annie and me? The road we'd travelled the last three years had been pretty rough.

So, what did you think? she asked again. Maybe you thought Larry might have found himself a younger woman? Or maybe you thought I was dead? Did you think I was dead, Axel?

I could hear her breathing at the other end of the line. She sounded asthmatic.

Did you?

No, I said quickly. No. None of those. I don't know what I thought. The lie seemed the wise way to go. Easier. I turned and looked through the bevelled glass of the entrance. Moonlight filtered through the tall firs and lit the rose garden with a blue glow. It was a cool light for such a warm summer evening. The pathway leading to the Tea House looked mysterious and forbidden.

How are you Carla? I asked.

I'm fine, Axel. Just fine, she said. Nice of you to ask. I get around as best I can. You know how it is? We get older. She laughed. Right?

She stopped talking. Then I heard her moving. I heard the rustle of cloth.

She said, I was lying down when you phoned.

Sorry, I said. You should have told me. I didn't mean to wake you. I guess I wasn't thinking. I didn't check the time.

You didn't wake me, she said. I'm glad you called. I still have to rest a lot. Sometimes I have to lie down for days on end. You know what it's like when you can't move? Nothing will stay still.

The Last Time We Talked

I could hear her laughing and wheezing at the other end of the line.

She said, Then I get this overwhelming urge to move. God I hunger to move. To run. Or, better still, fly. I'd like to walk in space. Do you know what I mean, Axel? Not to have to depend on anything or anyone for help? That's what I wish for when they tell me I have to rest. I want to move. Not lie here like I'm a goddamn corpse.

That doesn't sound so good, I said.

We all need our beauty rest, Axel. Some just need more than others. At least that's what they tell me. She laughed again. Her voice softened when she said, It's good to hear your voice, hon. How are you doing?

I'm all right, I said. What else could I say? I said, I'm almost fifty. Remember when we used to joke that we'd be lucky if we made it to fifty?

Yes, she said. You were going to come to some dramatic end. In a racing car or at the top of some godforsaken mountain in the middle of the Himalayas. Good Christ, Axel, you used to get dizzy climbing a ladder.

This time when she laughed, she also snorted. Carla was enjoying herself at my expense. The sounds she made with her nose annoyed me.

I remember, I said, I remember. We were just kids. Give me a break. Anyway, unless I get hit by lightning, which seems about as likely as some quack writing me a prescription for whiskey, I'll be fifty in two months. Less a couple of days. But who's counting.

When I finished talking I could hear movement at the end of the line, but I sensed no one was listening. Carla, I said, you there? No one answered. Shit, I said. Carla, don't play games with me. Answer me, you hear? Larry? I pressed the phone into my ear until it hurt. Larry, you there? What's going on? Larry, answer me, I yelled. I turned to see the warden look out of her office down the hall towards me. She put a fat finger to her colourless lips and disappeared.

Part of me wanted to shout into the bitch's face. Up close. The other part of me was beginning to panic when I heard Carla say, Larry's asleep, Axel. It's late. We have separate rooms.

Where the fuck you been? I said.

I had to move, she said. Larry and I sleep apart so I won't wake him. My hours are quite irregular. And, as I told you, I need to move. I'm fine now. Besides, Larry has to go into the office in the morning.

What office? I asked. What's he doing these days?

The car dealership, she said. Didn't I say. She paused. Sorry, Axel, I thought I told you. Larry's a partner in a car dealership.

I thought only politicians owned car dealerships, I said. I tried to kill the snide tone but Carla picked up on it.

Cute, Axel, she said. Cute. Where are you staying?

I twisted the phone cord around my fingers. I'm at the Redwood Center, I said.

The detox place? Carla said. I could hear the surprise in her voice.

Not to worry, I said. I'm in the advanced stages of cure. I'm really here for the R & R. I wanted to joke about it but the jokes were all stale.

You're a boozer, Axel, she said. If you're staying at the Redwood Center, you're a boozer. There is no cure, Axel. You just can't drink.

No, I said. I know that.

I wanted to tell her that I hadn't had a drink now for a month. At the beginning, the days blurred into one another a bit. I wanted to tell her about my mood swings. It was the mood swings I couldn't control.

Axel, she said, you need to talk to Larry.

Why is that? I asked. But I got the sense she was thinking of something else.

He can help you, she said. Believe me. He can help you, she said.

I wanted to ask her what special knowledge Larry had, but she said, I got to go Axel. It's late. I'll tell Larry you're here. He'll call and arrange to meet with you. I'd like to come along but I don't think they'll let me out. Not at the moment. She sounded breathless. Distant.

Carla, I said. But I heard the clock at the other end of the line. Outside, the moon was half hidden behind a bank of cloud. The path was barely visible. Shadows moved like animals stalking the garden. For the first time in a long while I felt vulnerable. Afraid.

That had been two nights ago.

Since then I'd been to three sessions conducted by the warden, Mrs. Phyllis Staunton. She was tough, but I found I could open up to her. She didn't pry. She didn't nag or accuse. That's what I disliked the most. The accusations. With her I found myself talking, telling her things I'd never revealed to anyone else.

Annie and I always ended up screaming at each other. Insulting each other. Soon I was throwing things. Grabbing people. Hitting people I loved.

Phyllis said that was often the way we were. Men who drank. I'd be that way, she said, until I got the bug out of my brain. Nothing excused my behaviour, she said, but it might help me to understand myself. To know that I was ill. I had to get rid of my guilt. This was the kind of shit I'd always figured was liberal double talk. Weakness mistaken for sickness. But I was at the point of revising that view.

When Larry had phoned and asked me out to lunch, Phyllis went all soft at the mention of his name. This short, chunky woman who wore a grey wool suit on the hottest of summer days actually flushed in the cheeks when she heard the name of Larry McCormack.

Then she stammered that of course I could have the afternoon off – that an afternoon with Mr. McCormack would do me a world of good. That there were few men as fine as Mr. McCormack.

And after all he has been through, she said.

The way she spoke, I thought I was going to lunch with a saint.

We have ordered lunch.

From the terrace I look out to the bay. Two sailboats ride at anchor. Larry hasn't said much since he gave me the tour of the dealership. I'm impressed. It's a sizeable operation. A lot of responsibility, I say, although I still find it hard to believe that anyone I know could be hawking cars for a living. I'd always thought of it as a profession for desperate men. He stares at me and I can only retreat to the bay and mountains beyond.

When I swing my head back, Larry is still studying me as if I'm a goddamn specimen on a slide. So I continue turning and look into the window at our reflection. Truth is, Larry looks a lot better than I do. He has a latin complexion, a black beard which is peppered with just the right amount of grey, and a head full of silver hair. He's tall and has no gut to speak of. The tan slacks and blue and green checked sports shirt fit him as though a tailor's life had hung in the balance. He exudes confidence. Perfection. I feel anxious, keyed up, ready to spring. Then I see his lips move. I turn and look at the table in front of him.

You listening? he asks.

I nod.

Do you beat up on Annie? he says.

I want to protest. This is nuts. I didn't come out to lunch to be interrogated about my private life.

Do you? he insists. One thing I now remember about Larry is that he can be relentless.

Yes, I say. I mean, I used to. I haven't in a while, I say.

And the kids? he says. You do have kids?

Yes, I say.

Well, he says.

I give him a puzzled look. I want to divert his attention away from wherever he's taking us. When I look at him, his eyes give me the creeps.

Do you smack them around, too? he says.

I was crazy then, Lar. I didn't know what I was doing. I love them all, I say.

I'm about to crack. I can feel the tears in my eyes. I'm tempted to order a beer. I used to tell myself that one beer was not like an ounce of whiskey. I used to be able to divide my life up like that. Into parts, separate from each other.

I say, More often than not spanking them was a matter of discipline. A way of keeping order in the household, I say.

Don't bullshit me, Axel, he says. Don't try to con the master.

We stare hard at each other. I want to tell him to get out of my face. He's beginning to smother me. There is an edge to his voice. My legs feel numb.

I turn away. I watch a gull swoop down and pull a shell out from between the rocks and barnacles.

After you moved, he says, after you moved, it took the doctors another two years to diagnose what was wrong with Carla. Her skin would turn and then heal. Turn and heal. They found out that her circulatory system hadn't developed properly. Blood wasn't getting to her hands and feet. Then the problem extended to her arms and legs.

The gull lifts off the ground, flies to thirty, maybe forty, feet.

He says, Then came the surgery. Four major surgeries on her nervous system. They needed to kill the signals being sent by the brain to the nerves that control the blood supply. Four major operations over two years. Three were relatively successful. She still needed to lie down, though. That's the only way her heart would pump blood to her whole body. And when she was lying down the pain subsided. But the fourth operation didn't work. Lesions kept appearing on her left arm. And they were growing larger and becoming infected.

The gull faces into the prevailing wind, glides and drops the shell. I hear the smack on the rocks, like a fist on flesh, and then watch the bird drop out of the sky to the beach, its beak pulling the guts out of the broken shell. I've always been squeamish. I want to tell him to stop. I've heard enough.

But he continues. The infection she has right now, he says, covers an area about this size. He uses his index finger to drawn an imaginary line around his shoulder and down his chest. He traces back and forth over the line where Carla's breast would be.

Jesus Christ, Lar, I say. I had no idea.

She could die at any time, he says.

What confuses me is that I can hear no remorse, no distress in his voice. I'd be a basket case if it were Annie.

The sun pushes up above the trees. Soon we're feeling the full blast of the noonday heat.

How do you deal with it? I ask. Everything I'm thinking sounds trite.

Carla taught me. He pauses and folds his table napkin. Precisely, from corner to corner. We're dealt a hand, he says. Right?

I nod.

We can't change that hand, either. You understand? The timer's on.

That's a little too fatalistic for me, I say.

Don't be a dummy, Axel. Listen to me. Listen carefully.

I want to run. Larry's mad. I want to tell him my fate is to run when I hear this kind of talk. But I'm stuck in my seat.

He says, After Carla's last operation I looked forward to see what my prospects were. I saw *nada*. Only a lot of suffering. And I looked backwards to see if I could figure out what I'd done to deserve this. To love someone as much as I do and then to have to watch her in this kind of pain, well that was more than I could bear. So I drank. I began and ended my days with gin. That was easy. Gin was something, the one thing, I could count on.

What happened? I asked.

I quit, he says.

You quit, I say. Just like that! You quit. What am I supposed to do, get down on my knees?

I live from day to day, he says. No magic.

Swell, I say. The breeze has picked up off the water. I can feel the perspiration drying on my forehead. Is that it? Is this all Phyllis's guru has to offer?

And Carla? I ask. What about Carla?

He smiles. Well, every so often, he says, I take a pillow and place it over her head. Usually in the morning, after coffee, just before I head off for work.

What? I say.

When I press down, he says, she wakes up. She thrashes her legs and arms around a bit. Then in a muffled voice, she says, That you, Lar? Honey, that you? Yes, I say, yes it is dear. And she says,

The Last Time We Talked

Tempted again are you? Then we both laugh. A belly full of laughs, he says.

You're sick, I say. This is morbid stuff, Lar. People are committed for talking like this.

Then she tells me, he says, not today. All right, Hon? Someday sweetie, she says to me. Someday. But please not today, she always says.

He is on the verge of crying. Up in the trees the crows are talking to each other. I remember one day, when Annie and I were arriving home, seeing two crows at the top of our driveway, one with its wing spread over the other.

Do you know what you're saying? I ask.

Yes, he says. Yes I do.

What? I say.

Love, he says.

But I can't figure if what he's said is a question or an answer.

BLÁNAID MCKINNEY

The Gold of Tolosa

Linda punched the intercom and said 'Okay Robert, how about this? One shot each of genuine gold-flake whiskey, vermouth and a touch of soda, with lots of crushed ice, in a nice, fat, chunky glass.'

Robert smiled to himself. Last week it was famous Canadians, this week it was the creation of a new cocktail, next week it would probably be her collection of Tex Avery cartoons, edited together for the staff during lunch hour. Robert's personal favourite was her scale outline of the U.S.S. Starship Enterprise 1701-D, superimposed over an O.S. 1:2500 map of the city. The damn thing covered most of Crouch End.

He liked Linda's clever enthusiasms and had never comfortably regarded her as his secretary, especially as she had travelled a great deal, and yet embraced her clerical job in the Environmental Health Department with the same unselfconscious, kind energy with which, he had come to learn, she approached everything. She didn't make him feel unsophisticated and he was grateful to her for that. 'Oh! Bob, listen, by the way – are you free this afternoon for a site visit? Graham just called in. His pumping station meeting is overrunning and there's no way he'll make it back before five.'

'Okay, okay, who and where?'

'It's an old lady in Cecile Park. She just wants some advice about clearing out old furniture and whatnot. Big house. Been there for years, so God knows what she's collected. Come on, you heartless sod, go and say hello to a little old lady. Oh, and the garage called. They've finished the service, but there are a few bits and bobs needing done. That'll be another couple of hundred quid, eh?'

It was gently raining. On the bus, he sat behind a black girl in a bright African dress who'd hauled herself noisily up the steps. Her hair was webbed by thousands of tiny raindroplets, which sparkled dully in the electric light. Robert stared at the back of her head and thought about his wife, and about how much better it would have been if someone had turned up in mourning colours other than black – the deep blue of ancient Rome, the bright yellow of Egypt and Burma, Iranian beige, Korean white, the mad scarlet of Celts and gypsies.

His throat tightened slightly. He concentrated hard on the damp halo in front of him, its amicable bounce, on two boys in front, all denim and elbows, on the blundering sparrows outside in the dusk.

The rain dribbled slowly down the bus window, melting the orange street lamps beyond. Robert knew that, in a city, lights that threw no shadows were necessary, but he hated them; if a migraine could have a shape it would be like that, a chic, bright wound.

The bus was filling up with the Friday night pussycats. That's how he thought of them, the urban environmentalists, in their lunatic colours and perilous hairstyles. Robert wore navy or brown, but he enjoyed having something interesting to look at. One couple looked nice. The boy, a handsome Indian lad with letters shaved into the sides of his head (Robert couldn't make it out), wore a magnificently sloppy red T-shirt, with the Silver Surfer on it, cycling shorts and huge Doc Martens. His girlfriend looked like an oriental Clara Bow, a diminished, soiled little ghost in grey lace, pale make-up and spectacular South American earrings. As they got up to leave, the boy turned, taking her elbow in a delicate, gentlemanly way, and Robert saw that his hair said 'SKUNK.'

Others took their place. A serene, beautiful teenage boy with one fingernail painted gold, a collection of girls, quite drunk, shrieking, and finishing each others' sentences, with roars and muscular whoops and magazines of laughter. Just past Finsbury Park, a weary man in a navy suit climbed heavily into a seat, and for half an hour stared at the back of Robert's head. The dessicated cyphers of North London streamed wetly past in elongated cameos. A young woman got on with two children. She had a look of sad, fierce thrift about her; Robert noticed her lean, muscled forearms, as if she worked out. Like Madonna, he thought. Her children were very well behaved, and chatted to each other in scorched, prayer-like whispers while she stared distantly out the window, trailing the odd dreaming finger across their heads. He'd lived here all his life yet had rarely failed to be overwhelmed by something as basic as a bus ride. The fact that it all worked. So many miracles of purpose. The million tiny crimes, the sticks-and-stones civility, the palpable intelligence in the city's spine. The fact that it can't possibly work, yet did.

The house was late Victorian, and had a slovenly look of historical sneakiness to it, as if the builders had changed their minds, half way through. Robert liked the pale, warm brickwork, though, and the frozen calligraphy around the door. He had briefly trained as architect a long time ago, before giving up when the money ran out. But he still took an interest and, when walking around town, tended to look like a confident tourist, his gaze always fixed at a point somewhere above the shop fronts. He loved the tatty snobbery of some buildings, the injured hooliganism of others, those parts of the city like a collapsed scrum, where there was barely enough time before the developers moved in to find out which neck had been broken, which Georgian or Edwardian urban harpy had been ruined, or scalped beyond saving.

He laid his left palm against the pearl brick and pressed the doorbell again. There was no answer. He pushed the door and took a couple of cautious steps inside.

The place was like a bombsite. Hulking pieces of ancient furniture lay everywhere, some upended.

He wandered about in silence, wondering where the old lady was. He tried the other rooms. One room was bare apart from three enormous, five-foot tall potted plants in the centre of the floor. Robert stared at them. They were marijuana plants.

The walls were festooned with very old, enamel and metal Underground and street signs. 'Stroud Green Road', 'Panton Street', 'St. Augustine's Avenue', 'Kings Cross'. Dozens, perhaps hundreds of them, from all parts of the city. They were in pristine condition. Probably worth a fortune, thought Robert. Probably stolen too.

He found the bedroom. She was lying on the bed. He stared at her for a while. He knew she was dead. He checked her pulse. She

The Gold of Tolosa

was dead. He stared at her face. He knew this old woman. He'd spoken to her, months ago, at the local pub quiz. She was having tea and a sandwich on a beautiful Saturday afternoon, not taking part, but listening to the questions. What was 'The Gold of Tolosa?' No one knew. Robert didn't know, but he was sitting near her and had watched her. Her expression had changed slightly and the pale blue of her eyes reflected a colour that came from a long way away, from centuries ago, as she struggled to remember. Her voice echoed a soft classroom mantra.

'The Gold of Toulouse. Caepio. Caepio and Maximus. 106 B.C. Their army desecrated the temple of the Celtic Apollo. They stripped it of its gold, its jewels, and mocked the God. But the Apollo of the Celts exacted a terrible revenge and placed the howling Cimbrians in their path. One hundred thousand men died on that battlefield. They all died. Caepio and Maximus. 106 B.C. The Gold of Tolosa.'

She blinked.

'Ill-gotten gains never prosper, I suppose. The ultimate security is to possess nothing worth stealing.'

Everyone had looked at her.

Robert got up and sat down beside her. They had talked for a little while. He'd told her that his wife was ill. She told him about her dead husband, Jack.

'Jack was a couple of years younger than me,' she murmured. 'He was a collector, I was a scavenger. There's a big difference, but we got along fine in Dublin. I was studying classics at Trinity, but I was dying to go to New York with him. He had some strange jobs before Exxon took him on in the 1950's. He even worked at a TV station, as a scorekeeper on a quiz show. But they fired him.'

'What happened?' Robert found himself saying.

'He got plastered one night and racked up 250 points for the biggest moron the show had ever seen. The studio audience damn near lynched him,' she laughed, 'But the moron took us both out for a fine dinner.'

Robert smiled. 'You seem to have had fun together.'

'Yes, a lot of fun.' She talked a little more about her Jack, jobs he'd had, places they had lived. Her voice had a svelte, otterish quality, with traces of different accents surfacing and receding as she spoke. 'We once got arrested for dancing on McCarthy's grave.'

Robert blinked in confusion. 'The puppet?'

'Ha! No, the patriot, or at least that's what he called himself.'

Robert had always wanted to go to America. Mainly to look at the buildings, but he was also fascinated by the idea of a people whose spatial sense was so different from his own. To drive across the mid-west for hundreds of miles, and see nothing but horizon. And to hear only the graceful patois of the Plains. He knew it was all rubbish. He knew that the unimaginable spaces were becoming imaginable and manageable, filled up with features that in dot-to-dot fashion would slowly chase the loneliness of such places. He knew that the middling drawl of Kansas, after three weeks, probably bounced off the ear no more attractively than the glottal stops of South London. He knew that he wanted to have it both ways, so he had never gone.

'Do you miss him?' He couldn't believe he'd asked her that. 'I'm sorry, I didn't mean to pry. Sorry.' There was something about her vagrant yarns, the casual tetch and shrewdness of her voice, something that made him want to know more about her.

'Who, Senator McCarthy?'

'Eh, No, no, Jack, your husband.'

'No. I don't miss him.' She had waggled a translucent, mesmerising knuckle at him. Her voice was utterly level. 'Oh, don't misunderstand me, I loved him dearly. We were together a long time, but after three heart attacks, the fun and the dog-dancing and the shine on things just doesn't come back. Besides, he wasn't in pain. I'd say he had a very reasonable death. I've never been lonely or bored in my life.'

A reasonable death.

He hadn't asked her name.

He backed out of the bedroom in a kind of terror and walked slowly around the living room, touching the furniture. A job where he could use his hands, yes. He remembered how as a boy he'd wanted to be the best pickpocket ever. He would always have given the wallet back, of course. Or someone who makes children's pop-up books. A skill.

'No ambition, that's your problem,' his mother had said, with authentic bitterness.

When his wife had cried, four months ago, he tried to comfort her by appearing to be affected in a manner people seemed to find more acceptable, by what? Moving down a gear? But she saw through his solemn, shy tableau after a couple of days, and he ended up feeling like an unconsenting donor. He tried a consoling brand of romance, only to be depressed by the careless impoverishment of the language. Flowers, dinner, candles. The most romantic thing Robert had ever seen was the shabby, lichen-covered grave of a seventeenth century Aberdeen butcher, with a skull and crossbones carved on the table-stone, accompanied by grotesque worn reliefs of the tools of the man's trade – axe, cleaver, knife, and the stern message 'Memento Mori'. A holiday. He suggested going to the snow sculpture contest in Finland, held in January. Something unusual, and beautiful. And skilled. To spend a long weekend watching thirty huge, bearded Rodins creating astounding structures with pick axes and blow torches and chainsaws; she didn't say no. She just stared at him.

Dinner, then, in a nice restaurant, and a fragile, injured night it was. She was looking so pretty, so much younger. When she smiled and said in a fake Brooklyn bimbo accent that she was just going to 'fix her face', he asked her if she knew the origins of lipstick; she said no and her face set in a slightly preparatory way. Lipstick, he told her, in what he thought was a joking tone, was used by prostitutes on the streets of ancient Rome to indicate a willingness (for extra denarii, of course) to perform fellatio. Her expression didn't change. She just stared at him. 'Thanks Bob,' she had said in a voice that raked his heart, and raised his neck hairs. He didn't know. He had no idea she was feeling so bad. And then she lowered her eyes and actually blushed. They had been married for sixteen years. That was another one of Linda's gems.

Everyone had said she was brave, towards the end. Perhaps she was. Robert didn't understand the process whereby disease transformed an embattled, clever, snobbish, substantially ordinary woman into a saint. He suspected that it was for the benefit of others, that few people are authentically courageous, but we must convince ourselves that they are. Besides, he hadn't been that involved. There had sprung up legions of people, mostly women, to look after her, to organise everything. His sister – it was as if the job of coping, the business of unfussy practicalities had fallen to her as naturally as rain. Robert had gradually and, over the months, helplessly, assumed the demeanour of a listless squaddie standing around a bomb site, watching the disposal experts, waiting for something to detonate, hoping it wouldn't. He had welcomed casual exclusion when it happened, all his life. What use would he have been? He was no good at the warm, tawdry engagements of the whole business. It wasn't a crime to grieve properly. No one was forcing him to rush from catastrophe to instant forbearance, the way bereaved parents of murdered children look on television. He hadn't planned it like that. He hadn't meant to be stoically frozen, he simply was unsure as to how he was supposed to behave. In a small way, he resented those who showed it the luxury of their – what – self indulgence? No. But he knew he was not cold. At least he hoped he wasn't. He didn't know what kind of comparison to make. He didn't know whether he would go twelve rounds, because he'd never gone near the ring. Very slowly, very slowly, it occurred to Robert that his mother had perhaps meant, not ambition, but something else. Something requiring a little colour and arrogance and effort from his ignorant heart. It occurred to him that, all his life, his mother had been calling him a coward.

In the bathroom, there was a tiny rectangular wooden frame, propped up by the sink, with a quotation in Spanish and, underneath, a translation – 'Que los yerros de amores, dignos son de perdonar'. Faults of love deserve to be forgiven. A feeling of something like misery rose in his chest and subsided, and he forgot for a moment to breathe. He moved to the kitchen in a dreamy march. There was a half-bottle of whiskey on top of the fridge. He poured himself a large one, went to the living room and sat heavily on the floor beside the window, his briefcase on his knees. He felt

The Gold of Tolosa

as if he was disappearing, as if the room was slowly, sponge-like, drawing the energy from him. His chest felt crushed, his throat paralysed. He wished he'd told a few glossy lies in his life. He closed his eyes, and saw his wife's dead countenance, glamorous and totemic, and the grieving criminal germs of memory crept up on him.

She'd been afraid to die and she didn't hide her fury at first. But the silent, desperate need for heroism broke her; the weakness of the embarrassed, the healthy, the solicitous, was too much for her. She was not permitted to behave badly. She was afraid to die but that was okay. She wasn't afraid to live; Robert remembered the time she'd disappeared for three days. He had reeked of anxiety, and cried hysterical tears when she had strolled, mad-eyed, in the front door, carrying a bottle of expensive perfume, her handbag jangling with French francs. She never ran away again. The years made her polite.

There must be sins greater than cowardice, but the constant insult of her disreputable courage had stung him always. It was not coldness that had battened down the hatches, it was bad manners. Robert made as if to laugh and it emerged as a desolate, dirty sob. He lowered his head into his hands and cried in utter silence like an exhausted, famished child. The grief rose up and battered at him for several minutes.

Gradually, his breathing returned to normal. He gripped his briefcase and blinked at the opposite wall, in genuine surprise. He didn't know whether he felt better or worse.

There was an almost imperceptible scratching noise from the attic. Robert looked up. A mouse, probably. He let his mind wander. He couldn't be bothered anymore. He thought about the genetically engineered Oncomouse in America, a poor creature whose only function was to develop tumours for laboratory examination, and then die, but not before producing similarly cursed offspring. Had it be patented? He couldn't remember. He was very tired. What had the old lady called her husband, whom she loved dearly? – 'illustre sconoscinta' – an illustrious nobody. Fine.

He stood up and looked out at the street lighting, eyeing the stupidity of moths, holding his glass up to the light, and tried to imagine gold flake floating, darting like gypsy shoals, like bog rain, like the flittering stony follicles of granite buildings that made parts of the city twinkle after a wet spell.

He thought of the roomful of signs. King's Cross. The man whose body was never identified, never claimed, even after computer enhancement and the pathologists' patient detective work. Suddenly energetic, he went to the bare room and took a cutting, with roots, from one of the marijuana plants. He took one of the signs from the wall, his beloved Frank Pick's Underground 'bullseye' motif, and put them both into his briefcase. He would put it in his bathroom, the way students displayed stolen traffic cones.

For a little while he held the dead woman's cold hand. Then he headed for the phone.

DAVID BROWN

Off

He lost his balance momentarily, as the train lurched over a new section of track. He could usually read the rails and maintain his equilibrium, anticipating their curves and anomalies, bracing himself with his good leg as he dispensed tickets and change and banter to the passengers. He was surprised to find himself off kilter, falling sideways, grappling for support, grabbing the shoulder of the boy riding backwards at the end of the carriage. The boy raised his lashes from his book and fixed him with such an ice blue blaze of pity and contempt that the joke, something about 'guard caught off guard', froze in his throat.

'Sorry,' he muttered. 'I'm sorry,' and softly closed the door behind him as he escaped into the next carriage silently cursing the schoolboy and his privileged education and the supercilious uniform that permitted him to look up with such unequivocal composure.

He had finally formed a fairly good rapport with the boys from the private college. After an initial period of terrorisation, he had managed, with his quiet, jaunty wit and deadpan delivery, to parry the jokes about his leg and the threadbare, ill fitting uniform and the comic opera hat he was compelled to wear. He had established a tentative camaraderie and when they stormed shouting onto the train, stinking of young sweat and hot tweed, he could greet some of them by name and keep most of them at bay. But he secretly hated their loud, pompous declamations, their cruel bullying and the impunity of their constant derision of the other passengers – plebs and poofs, slags and sluts. He tried to imagine them relegated to a position of subservience but it was difficult to divest them of their charmed arrogance and surety of purpose.

For some reason he steered as clear as he could of the blond boy with the arctic eyes; he would wordlessly clip the ticket the boy withdrew from a leather wallet initialled in gold and, unsmiling, the boy would sometimes look up, sometimes not, and each time their eyes met, a chill passed over the guard. The boy always sat alone, riding backwards, reading. Whenever he could, he chose a different carriage, or sat as far as possible from his roistering compatriots. The guard felt a small spasm of empathy, for often he would find himself, in the guards' van or in the cafeteria, separated from the other guards and clerks and the rowdy card playing maintenance men, buried in a book.

He had worked on the trains for nineteen years, since he was forced to get a job when his father went. But before that he had always enjoyed riding on them. He was soothed and at the same time aroused by the flow of the rails, the rhythmic swaying, the benign, sexual power of the locomotive and even as a boy he discovered that there was always one beauty in each carriage. He would search for that person and take ownership of them. And if the paragon proved elusive he would select parts of people – a beautiful neck, a seraphic pair of eyelashes, a hand resting eloquently on the seat-back – and assembly them in his imagination. Now when he played this game he found he always had to veto the schoolboy with the glacial gaze.

Since leaving school he was determined to compensate for his abbreviated education. He read passionately and indiscriminately, often late into the night and sometimes he became disturbed by the intensity and diversity of his reading. He would put down a book of Restoration comedies, pick up a computer manual describing the breathtaking implications of the Information Superhighway and he would lie back, listening to his mother wheezing in her sleep in the next room, wondering whether the shelves of his brain would be able to contain it all or if, one day, he would wake to find everything shredded, scrambled into a gibbering alphabet soup. And it was at times like these, when he needed to relieve the indigestion of his overfed mind, he would tiptoe into the living-room with a length of toilet paper and the video cassette he kept locked in a suitcase at the back of his closet. Running it silently on fast forward, he would bathe in the ambient oranges and blues and interleave himself with the thrashing limbs and the fleeting, spurting penises of his dreams.

Off

One afternoon, he was shouting directions to a short tempered, blue haired woman with a faulty hearing aid when the schoolboys roared onto the train. It was a sullen, windy day. The mutinous boys were mercilessly punching and jibing at each other and he steeled himself for a barrage of abuse. He forced his way down the aisle between the crowded seats, clipping their reluctant tickets, stepping over the bags and legs angled in front of him and opened the door into the next carriage.

Two boys with angry, red, Beethoven faces had the blue-eyed boy pinned over the back of the seat. One had an arm locked around his neck and the other was twisting his fist up behind his back.

'Say it', they were shouting. 'Say it you little homo. Say you want to suck it.' A single tear ran down the boy's face. His upper teeth were biting shut his lower lip.

'Get off,' the guard said, in a low even voice. 'Get off and leave him alone, you little pricks. And don't let me see you on this train again. Ever.' Slowly they let the boy go with a final, brutal shove and slouched off into the other carriage muttering 'We'll fix you gimp,' and 'fix you good, gimp poof,' and then erupting into a manic gale of artificial laughter.

The boy made no attempt to conceal the tears coursing down his pale cheeks. The guard quietly picked up the book that lay on the floor, dusted it on the seat of his pants and laid it on the seat next to the boy. The title on the cover was 'The Thief's Journal'. He limped out the back door of the carriage, through the guards' van and stood trembling on the small parapet at the back of the train. He looked down at his white knuckles gripping the balustrade and at the two blue rails unreeling beneath him, like twin destinies.

The boy wiped his face and put the book into his bag. He feared he was being hurtled into a future with no brakes and no emergency cord. He felt older than his fourteen years and at the same time felt unborn, as though he was about to emerge from the chrysalis phase of an unknown and terrifying life cycle.

He had just discovered the writing of Jean Genet in the Public Library where he spent the afternoons waiting for his mother to finish work. He felt that he had been suspended over a hissing, seething pit. His sleepless nights were populated by pimps and crooks and sinuous transvestites and his daydreams haunted by their beautiful names: Querelle and Stillitano, Java and Divine, denizens of a slippery world that drew and repulsed him, like an accident he couldn't look away from.

Each morning he would wake bloodshot and rumpled, push aside the muesli and pour himself a trembling cup of black coffee, feeling as though he had been violated in some way during the night.

'Growing pains,' his mother said, eyebrows raised, observing her pale, gangling, troubled looking son, 'look at you, you're growing out of yourself.' And he would stumble into the bathroom, remove his pyjamas and examine in the mirror the mysterious infiltration of hairs across his young body.

Beneath the railway station there was a vast and cavernous public lavatory. Its walls and floors were covered in blue and white tiles, tattooed with graffiti and every drip, every footfall echoed and boomed. The sweet smell of urine was embittered with disinfectant. Along one wall, above the handbasins, there was a series of mirrors. With time they had tarnished and dimmed, returning a blemished and distorted reflection.

The guard took off his ridiculous cap, turned on the tap and rinsed his hands in the gushing, deafening flow. He stood thinking for a while, blanching his wrists in the icy water. He turned off the tap and jerked a towel down from its dispenser. The echo ricocheted off the tiles like gunshot. He ran his fingers through his red hair. It looked greenish in the subaqueous mirror and his sad, green eyes looked oxidized and foreign, shadowed with mauve. He felt in his back pocket for a comb, dipped it in the basin and dragged the hair back off his face. He was reaching for his cap when a crash rang off the walls, reverberating like a dropped gong. He looked up to see that one of the metal doors in the line of cubicles facing the washbasins had swung open, slammed open, and there, reflected in the wintry ocean of the mirror, stood the boy. The guard turned and before he could speak he was harpooned by those inevitable eyes. He heard the echo of his shoes on the unforgiving tiles as he was reeled in, the echo of the boy's schoolbag as it hit the floor and the echo of his beating heart.

Without a word the boy took the guard's cap from his hand, let it fall, opened the silver buttons of his uniform and charted with his lips the constellation of freckles from nipple to nipple. The man's hands rose, hovered like trembling birds just above the surface of the boy's hair, then dropped to his sides and then clenched as the boy released his belt and followed with his tongue a rivulet of sweat. Something blossomed and then bloomed deep inside the guard, an exquisite nausea, and he did not know whether its pressure would be unleashed from his own mouth or into the mouth of the boy.
The guard reached down to stroke the tender feathered neck. He took the boy's shoulders, gently raised him and, as he leaned down onto his mouth, he reached in and grasped the slim lever of the boy's cock.
'Get your hands off. Get your fucking hands off,' the boy hissed. He turned away, wiping his mouth with the back of his hand. He zipped his trousers, picked up his bag and walked out of the numb silence, up the resounding stairs, leaving the guard quaking, his hands pressed over his ears to staunch the echoes.

The bar stretched into infinity. Drinks kept landing in front of him until his mouth, his ears and his eyes were covered in fur. The sodden fur of drunkenness. And yet, clawing at the back of his brain, eating into the delirium, were the facts, the true facts of real life. The fact that he had missed his next shift; the fact that he was completely drunk; the fact that his mother would be keeping his dinner warm in the oven; the fact that he had allowed himself to touch a private schoolboy in the public toilet of the railway station. And, horrified, he kept reciting to himself, 'Let him not trespass. Let me not trespass against him.' And remembering how, when his grandmother had taken him to a Billy Graham revival, the evangelist had pronounced 'The Devil is in Your Hands' and how for days he had studied and studied his little hands, waiting for his sins to materialize, like handfuls of shit. And through the stew of booze the words of the boy: 'Get your hands off.' 'Hands off.' 'Off.' echoed and echoed.

The barmaid of the Station Hotel wondered about the guard as he reeled from the bar. She was an old-fashioned barmaid who took pride in her vocation and a genuine interest in her patrons. She had not seen that one before. Most of the others frequented the hotel sometimes before and usually after their shifts and, now that the hotel had become unfashionable, at the dead end of the city, they were often the only customers. She had come to know the drunks and the losers, the provocateurs and aggressors and spent hours listening to their yarns and their problems. Sometimes she felt like some kind of social worker or therapist.

'Sixty bucks an hour is what I should be getting for putting up with all you'se blokes bullshit,' she would say. Yet there was something about this guard with the crook leg and the nice green eyes that roused in her, not pity exactly, more concern. The way he had emptied that dangerous succession of drinks without a glimmer of enjoyment. The way he sat staring into his glass, as though searching for a solution or waiting for a revelation. And he didn't seem to know what to do with his hands.

As the guard staggered into the night, in a townhouse on the other side of the city, the boy was waking from a dream. A deep dream in which he was plunged into a stagnant, submarine world where succulent half-humans nuzzled and sucked at his naked skin, tumbled and buffeted him in a syrupy sea. And each time he came up for air, he was met by the troubled eyes and the outstretched hand of the railway guard, but before he could be pulled to safety, before he could be rescued, he was dragged back down into the simmering, noxious stew.

In the bitter yellow light from the lamp installed outside his window to keep night prowlers at bay, he reviewed his encounter with the green-eyed guard, and, opening the cabinet of his heart, discovered remorse. This time, his wanton game had misfired. That game of manipulation, coercion and seduction that he practised so dispassionately had rebounded and wounded him.

And, reaching down deep inside himself under the duvet, he touched the wound and resolved to make amends.

Bits of the sky are falling, the guard thought, as he limped across the lawn in front of the station. Over the city, across the navy blue sky, a shower of meteors rained down. He stopped to watch, listening to the primordial shunting and coupling of locomotives in the railway yard and suddenly, as though illuminated by the falling stars, in his brain, in his blood he understood what was going to happen.

He could hear the sound of the distant express sighing through the rails as he unbuttoned his jacket, carefully folded it and placed it beside the track. He took off his shoes and trousers and put them on top of the jacket. His socks and underpants. The guard looked down and he thought he could see the stigmata the boy had left on his pale flesh. And he traced the crucifix of guilt from nipple to nipple, from throat to crotch and then he lay down on the harsh gravel between the tracks, rested a wrist on each rail and waited for the train.

KEVIN PARRY

On the Edge

'Why?' there it is again, the agonising, unanswerable question which wells in every pair of eyes and throbs ceaselessly in my brain like a lunatic pulse. And along with it the phenomenon I have so often remarked since being in here. Perhaps it is merely an accident of the lighting. I've observed it in all my visitors and I see it again now, in my son. As the forehead tenses with the stress of emotion, creases with compassion and incomprehension, and the brows lower, shading the liquescent eyes from the light, the pupils dilate into enormous black pools. There is something disturbing about the autonomy of this reflex, combining the coldly mechanical and the inhumanly primitive, something sinister, manifesting the implacable force that drives protozoic organisms to couple or to swallow each other. How shocking it is now to note this function in my young boy, to see these primitive black lagoons in the delicate unblemished innocence of his face. The pupils dilate with the unspoken question, and I stare into them, into eyes that seemed so familiar, and it is like standing on the edge of a crater, staring down into primeval darkness. They could be the eyes of a beast, a dog, an ape, regarding me, reflecting me. Depthless black, blank holes. Like the eyehole on the door. Like the barrel of the gun. Like the clotted velvet hole a gun makes.

And what is it they see, these pupils focused on me? A loving father, a generous friend, a considerate employer? The loved, sensitive features, so familiar, yet strange, jolted askance in the memory by this staid environment; the skin pallid under the bald lights; the stature attenuated by the vacuous anaemia of the room; the habitually kind, sincere mien disjointed by circumstances into half-remembered fragments from a dream? Or is it an absolute stranger they see? Peering down into the craters of my own pupils, do they dredge the black depths for the remains of the man they knew, scan the impenetrable surface for bubbles, for bits of flotsam to identify me by? Anything to answer the question, 'why?'

On the Edge

But there is nothing there, nothing. They are right to use blinding lights for interrogation, to pull tight the noose of the iris, to strangle the pupils' apertures to a reptilian pinprick, for nothing rises to the surface of those black pools. I shut my eyes tight, put my hands over them; the gauzy after-image of my son's pale face glimmers for an instant on the retina and sinks irretrievably down the dark fathoms. For memory is an unreliable dog, recalcitrant, devious, half-lame, retrieving what is closest to hand, limping back with the wrong things, disappearing for ages and returning with nothing. Nothing to answer the question. Again and again my brain raps out the command, 'Why? Why?'; but always it is the same inconsequential images that are dropped at my feet, the same tatters of conversation. Shuffle and splice them in a hundred thousand permutations, there is nothing to sublimate the unexceptional – no dramatic lighting, no subtle symbolism, no repressed trauma: always the final cut is a bland retrospective of an average life, sepia with ordinariness. Nothing to explain the last unexpungeable frames, that horrific, unreal, ridiculous sequence which has somehow attached itself to my life. And with what rabid obsessiveness are those images retrieved and replayed, backwards, forwards, slow-motion, double-speed, or laid freeze-frame before me: the long platform, the blue sky, the frantic rhythm of the figure in the wide and silent road, the snap recoil of my wrist, the circular pivoting of the body on the tar as the legs kick together, rabbit-like, the small still bundle of rags, the staring black eyes filmed over like stagnant pools, flecks of dust on the surface.

Absurd, outrageous images! Against them, night and day, I have battered myself bloody, but can neither dislodge nor disown them; they are mine. But the callous impulsive brutality that produced them! I *am* that stereotype, a quiet, mild, sensitive, generous man; no one who knows me would disagree. How can I ever accept or explain the emanation from within me of such horrendous whimsical psychopathy? The psychologist taps his pencil against his teeth and clutches at straws: he probes here and there without conviction: childhood, war experience, sexuality, racial orientation; but I can see him floundering. With the exception perhaps of particular success in business, the events of my life and my responses to them have been unexceptional, the common experience of most of my peers. He knows I have nothing to hide, no secret perversions, dark complexes or irrational manias that swing too far from the medial. I co-operate absolutely – desperately; raving in this horizonless desert I am far more eager than he to lift the rock under which hides the explanation of the inexplicable.

Pretorius his name is, but I don't really mind. He is young and educated and speaks English respectfully. It is his voice that asks the questions, not his eyes. Dark they are beneath his slim black eyebrows, dark and dull as tar, so that pupil and iris are barely distinguishable. And beneath the bronze of his skin, too, the umber lick of the brush they so fear and which seeps to the surface every couple of generations. They've all got it there somewhere. Like the captain who interrogated me – Engelbrecht – a wiry, brown little man with high cheek-bones and obvious reasons other than conservatism for keeping his hair so short. Quite commiseratory, he was, as though my crime made me one of them: 'Shoot 'em on your own property, Mr Harris, you're OK; but like this,' shaking his head dolefully, '*ja*, is not so good.' Pretorius, though, is non-committal, dispassionate, guarded. He has desisted from his original strategy of snapping out unexpected, unrelated questions, attempting to catch me unawares, hoping to bypass my command and trick the dog into betraying me, into digging up some tattered remnants of furtively buried motives. He now accepts my ingenuousness and has settled into a rather floundering cycle of re-examining previously covered ground. But there is, I perceive, something new in this approach: he has honed into fine prongs the distinguishing features of my crime and with these he probes various events and attitudes of my life for related responses – never mind full-blown motives, he would be happy with mere clues now. And so would I.

With one of the prongs he has, understandably, probed for the cold marble of psychopathy. But, other than that single anomalous act of brutality, I have no symptoms. I have never been impulsive, reckless or particularly short-tempered. Amongst the dredged-up memories and images of my early years he rummages fruitlessly for any childhood traumas or family instability which might have abraded or produced enduring contusions beneath the fragile skin of human sensitivity. Freely I give him the map of my childhood, the vast landscape of the Amatola foothills: lonely, lovely, sun-baked scrublands of grass and twisted thorn trees, prickly pears, huge flaming aloes, and the solitary winding thread of stony dust-track disappearing from sight many miles before reaching the blue creases of the surrounding hills. The Amatolas, blue as innocence, those lovely hills, Raphael-blue, folding gracefully down as the gown of a Madonna. And in her gentle lap the vast still vale where we finally settled on a smallholding after years of constant travelling between the scattered farms where my father found spells of work during the austere 1930s. A manager, my father was, forearms like clubs of oak, and never had to compete with blacks for work, as many of the 'poor whites' did. Them we passed on the roads, Afrikaners mainly, dirty ragged families of unsmiling dark-eyed children with insect-like limbs, living in upturned water tanks of rotting iron or makeshift sack tents. My parents struggled for many years, of course; our meals were frugal, our clothes patched and darned; I was teased at more than one school because I wore old boots that were too large and were laced with butchers' twine; but we were never 'poor whites'. Wherever we were my mother, as a matter of pride and morality, ensured that we always had a clean linen cloth and serviettes on our table, a manifest symbol of our family dignity and security that made a sanctum of the countless farmyard outhouses, sheds and dung-floored *rondawels* that were temporarily our home. Love radiated around that table as though it were a hearth, a glowing sun toward which our heads always faced.

But those dark petals of blood radiating from the clotted velvet receptacle, the viscous black corona that bloomed around his head on the tar, how did they grow out of the carefree glow of childhood innocence in the lap of the blue Amatolas? Where, on the immaculate white linen of my mother's tablecloth, was the blemish? Reading the starched expanse like a palm, following the lifelines of meticulously ironed folds, can the premonitory mulberry-dark stain be detected? Pretorius's shadowed eyes regard me dispassionately; but like mine, like my boy's, like all the eyes, they search for the hidden evidence, the washed-out, scrubbed-out, beaten-out, bleached-out ghost of an outline. And the dog works eagerly, snouting and rooting in the undergrowth of that childhood security and happiness; but the images dropped at our feet are few. Is there evidence of germinal psychopathy in these painful but isolated images? The image of my mother, following one of my father's occasional drinking excesses, sitting on the verandah steps, weeping, weeping, and I, hidden in the garden, too shocked and heartbroken at the sight of this proud woman broken down to comfort her – a fertile image to explain the origin of that touchstone of psychopathy, the incapacity for forming stable relationships, except for the fact that I was happily married for nearly twenty years until my wife's death from cancer. The image of the rabbit I brought down with my .22, its back legs frantically kicking together and I, fascinatedly watching the agonised pivoting towards death – a portentous early manifestation of callous bloodlust, except that I compassionately shot it again through the head to terminate its misery. These memories are infertile, experiences common to most children, yielding nothing to answer the question 'Why?'

Infertile, too, Pretorius's probing of subsequent years. My war experiences – unlike most *Afrikaners*, I cannot resist commenting to Pretorius, *I* volunteered – left scars, but no deeper than those suffered by most veterans. The usual nightmares that take sleep hostage or unexpectedly invade vacant waking moments forever after: the sickening gut-wrenching fear in battle, the clammy horror of death, the grotesque imagery of the strewn desert, the laughing faces and shattered corpses of departed comrades, the ignominy of Tobruk, the hunger of the Italian camps. The depression and sense of unregimented futility of the immediate post-war years were alleviated by my dedication, after a few false starts, to my job as a traveller for a general wholesaler servicing the rural Transkei with native merchandise – blankets, cloth, tin- and enamelware, ochre, beads, buttons, braid. Those thousands and thousands of miles of dirt-road that passed beneath my wheels, the red dust churning up in a cloud behind, hanging over the parched grasslands; those years of alternate weeks spent away from home, another deserted

On the Edge

Majestic or Royal or Imperial Hotel every night in another deserted one-horse town, sitting in empty bars staring at the White Horse and Brylcreem transfers stuck on the mirrors, playing game after game of snooker if there was a table; the rounds of calls on dusty trading stations, buzzing with flies and smelling of natives and horsedung, leather, dye, hessian and maize; the routine of jokes and sales patter to every trader. But selling! – the invigorating, ennobling challenge of selling! The art of presentation, the subtle expertise of flattery and persuasion, the electric charge of filling the order book, of topping last month's figures. This was my métier; almost every month's figures topped the last, year after year. Gradually, I became indispensable, powerful; no other traveller could hold a candle to my figures; I was liked and favoured by almost every trader in the area; the 'Blanket King', I was called; eventually I could demand terms from the wholesaler's directors. After fourteen years I became partner in a subsidiary company. Five years later I broke away and formed my own company. Within ten years of that I was a millionaire.

The habit of money-creation is still a driving force, the power of control, of employing people, the prestige of success, the respect it brings, but I have delegated and relaxed more over the last couple of years. I have a large, beautiful house with a neo-Grecian facade and swimming pool on top of a hill overlooking the river. So still and peaceful it is up there, above the bustle, the heat, the flies; isolated and peaceful. I have a plush XJ6 – I have always loved powerful cars. I play a lot of golf with a few select friends. I have never been a socialiser. I take pleasure in the quiet, simple things that wealth provides: the leisure to sit on my balcony, staring down at the wide brown river flowing with the tides, listening to classical music, playing chess, reading. At the age of fifty-five I have achieved all I want. I am content and relaxed, enjoying the days. Then one afternoon last week, without any thought, I shot a black child dead. He was about twelve years old. He has no name – his body has not been claimed.

Was it just a few days ago? Days and nights, minutes and hours, past and distant past seem all at time to contract into the immediate present and then recede absolutely beyond recall. It is the lack of sleep, the exhaustion, the relentlessness of thought, the indefatigable dog digging, digging, digging. My thoughts are scrambled, trip over each other. At least one or two of the images in every sequence belong elsewhere, belong to that afternoon. And with extra luminosity, in a sort of dreamlike surreality, they glow, like the fragmented floating stained glass facets of a Chagall window. But the sequence of that afternoon itself, summoned every hour, every half-hour, every few minutes, runs with perfect synchronism and absolute clarity of detail. Pretorius, too, has made me replay it several times, freezing it at various points to question me about the significance of certain details and what precisely was going through my head at the time. I know every individual frame, every detail of every frame.

Always it begins with me returning to the warehouse after lunch with Larry. We are going to meet at three-thirty for eighteen holes. As I turn the corner I see the boys offloading a large consignment of sugar, 750 bales, from a railway transport trailer that is parked at the rear door. Sipho, stripped to the waist, is on top, throwing the 25kg bales in a constant lift-and-pass rhythm to Mayekiso below who throws it in turn to the stacker just within the door. Hanging about around the side of the trailer is the usual gathering of ragged, snot-nosed piccanins. As I park the Jag behind the trailer I mutter a curse. Like bloody flies, they are, descending in little black swarms as soon as a delivery arrives, hoping to filch something off the side when anyone's back is turned. I get out and lock my door. They begin to straggle apart, ready to run, as they see me approaching. 'Go on!' I growl, swatting at them with my hand. '*Voetsek! Voetsek!* Go on, bugger off here!' They begin to run hesitantly, keeping their eyes fixed on me. I turn and call up to Sipho, 'You boys must watch these bloody *kwedins*, Sipho, hey?' He mumbles something in Xhosa. 'What?' I shout. 'Yes, baas, we watching them,' he replies, continuing to swing the bales. I turn around and see three or four of the beggars lingering on the edge of the pavement. I glare at them as I begin walking past the trailer to the front of the building. As I turn the corner some instinct makes me glance round again. I catch sight of one of them, taller than the rest and with a leer on his face, lifting his hand above his head in a swaggering motion of bravado. In it is a stone. I stop, stare at him for a few seconds, then turn and walk around the corner, climb the stairs onto the front loading platform and go into my office. I unlock my desk drawer, take out my revolver, click the safety catch off and walk back to the front door. Mrs Patterson sees the gun and stares at me. I walk along the loading platform. As I reach the stairs the group of piccanins saunters round the corner and sees me. The tall one is among them. I lift the revolver to eye level, arm locked at the elbow. With little panicked cries the group scatters. I watch only the tall one. He runs fast along the opposite pavement past the long front of the warehouse, never taking his eyes off me. Gaping black customers press themselves against the wall as I walk quickly along the long platform, trailing him until he has passed the glazed buildings on the other side of the road. He swings round the corner and careers down the middle of the empty road on its long decline toward the location. I stand at the end of the platform and watch the frantic rhythm of his pumping legs and flinging arms, rags of shirt slapping from side to side behind him. The sky is a perfect, unblemished Raphael-blue. I raise my locked arm, trap the bobbing figure between the walls of the sights and squeeze the trigger slowly. The crack of the shot and the snap of my wrist are instantaneous. The explosion seems to be at once within my skull and far off in the distance. There is a strange delay before it reaches the boy. Then, slowly, suddenly, awkwardly, his rhythm has faltered and he is down in the middle of the road, legs kicking rabbit-like together, his body pivoting like an insect on a pin. I wait a few moments till the movement stops and, under the aghast gaze of eyes from all sides, walk back along the long silent platform and through the warehouse to my office from where I phone the police.

I put a pin through a fly once. It spun round on the pin for a long time without dying, rotated so fast it was just a black blur. What is it that has pinned me here, spinning in these sterile circles of agony? Is it a misconception of myself, of who and what I am? One of Pretorius's newly-honed probes has disturbed me, touched its cold steel to a hidden nerve, exposed a jagged fissure in my understanding of myself. He asked me, simply, 'Would you have shot him if he had been white?' I was taken aback. Throughout this continuum of anguish it is not a question that has once presented itself. I shook my head in amazement, trying to dispel the extraordinary sudden fog so I could see. But the answer was absolutely clear: 'No,' I said, 'I wouldn't have shot him if he had been white: it would never have occurred to me. No.'

This revelation has perplexed me. Does it put me on a par with the likes of Engelbrecht, to whom the question never occurred either, amongst the splayed corpses on the streets of Mdantsane and Guguletu, astride the machine-gunned schoolchildren of Soweto? Am I a small-column news item indistinguishable from those Boers who routinely *sjambok*, bludgeon or shotgun their farm labourers to death? Shall I learn the *vastrap*, blow my nose in my hand, speak their guttural scullery-servant's tongue? What has abased me to the level of the brutal, uncouth killers of this country, slouching in their blue uniforms, smirking behind sunglasses, hands on batons, holsters gleaming? Am I, too, a henchman of these dour, granite-face neo-Nazis, black hats over black hearts, saluting their covenanted flag – these fanatic bastards who, while we were fighting up north in the name of democratic freedom, were skulking in alleyways with iron bars and swastikas? I have opposed them at every turn, chaining this country to their oxwagons and dragging it out of the Commonwealth back into that isolated, stunted hinterland of *Voortrekker* republicanism, reviled skunk of the world. De Villiers Graaff has been too soft, too much the gentleman against these devious *bywooners* whose funereal parliamentary suits can never disguise their coarse, questionable peasant stock, and the United Party is all but defunct. I shall vote Progressive in next year's elections. I have always admired Helen Suzman's lonely, courageous stand against these callous cultureless boors.

But the racial implication of my answer to Pretorius's question is incomprehensible. I have examined it from every angle, turning it over and over, like the strangely mottled stone I once found in my garden and sat for ages inspecting, trying to determine whether its tracery-like patterns were inherent compositional veins or the fossil imprints of some primeval life form. Blacks have been a general and mainly unobtrusive aspect of the landscape I've grown up and lived in. On the farms of my childhood there were always thatched huts down on the land somewhere, overrun by scrawny fowls and cowering mongrel dogs, where the labourers and servants squatted with their throngs of naked, pot-bellied children. A natural part – and, thinking back, rather a picturesque part, I suppose – of the backdrop to my years of travelling through the vast hut-speckled grasslands of the Transkei was the ochre-painted *gaba* women in their orange blankets and bangles, pails of water or bundles of firewood on their heads; white-blanketed *abakhwetha* boys, lonely ghosts of smeared white clay; tiny herdboys driving ox-sleds of plaited wattle; solemn greatcoated old men on horseback, holding up a palm in greeting; ragged piccanins with cupped hands at cattle-grids and gates, scrabbling in the dust for sweets, coins, cigarette butts. I knew the costume traditions – apparently, they all had some sort of symbolic significance – of every tribe and clan in the area. From a distance and at a glance I could tell the type of every garment they wore – the braided white kaffir-sheeting and white blankets of the Goaleka, the red-ochred shawls of the Tembu, the Reckitts-blued blankets of the Pondo, the bright orange of the Bomvana, the ubiquitous black cashmere *doeks* and shawls, towel babywraps, blue-print and panel-print skirts, melton headwraps. In fact, probably more than half of it reached their backs via my order book. But between these people and me there was, of course, never any sort of contact; I neither liked nor disliked them; they were, like the grass, the aloes, the cattle, simply part of the landscape I travelled through.

I suppose the only black I have known on any sort of personal level was Silas, my sample-boy for almost fourteen years. For many hundreds of thousands of miles he sat beside me in those big old V8 Dodges and Plymouths. He was seldom a problem – I never fraternised with him. Occasionally he and some of the other sample-boys got together in their outside quarters behind the hotels and drank too much. He would appear with violently bloodshot eyes in the morning, have little to say and nod off in the car. Not that we ever conversed, as such, though his English was fair – just the odd quip or comment, but mainly I listened to the radio. We were strangers, really, I suppose, sitting side by side for all those years but living in our separate worlds. I heard he died of T.B. a few years after I left; he was always thin as a rake and did, come to think of it, have a chronic hacking cough. A good boy, old Silas, always cheerful and polite.

Things have changed since those days. The old customs have gone. Even in the rural Transkei, now, traditional dress is a rarity. With homeland 'independence' imminent, most white traders have sold up to blacks and moved out. It is a ramshackle scene, the countryside, severely overpopulated, littered with the gutted carcasses of motorcars, men sitting around, the land eroded and untilled, people wandering aimlessly about. The old customs are gone; no wave now to the passing white motorist.

Here in the city, of course, things have always been different; the blacks are different. Much of the backdrop is familiarly unexceptional – lines of roadworkers swinging pickaxes in rhythm; gardenboys leaning on forks; uniformed maids polishing the red steps of verandahs or beating doormats; heaving, sweating hordes in the secondary commercial areas – but there is a sharp metallic sophistication about urban blacks, spawned in the vicious sprawling townships that seem to define every horizon, a tendency, not confined to blade-faced *tsotsis* slouching on corners, to observe expressionlessly out of the corner of the eye. But even here their ubiquitous presence has never really impinged on more than the margins of my consciousness, like the awareness, so vague as to preclude reaction, of the incessant buzzing of flies in the summer heat.

So what was it that suddenly pierced this membrane of habitual imperception, like a stab of intense light that snaps the iris into implacable focus? The raising of a hand in childish bravado? What obscuring film, smeared across my vision, deflected this image into the recesses of animal instinctuality? What distorting lens projected a child's fist in the form of a raised axe, a panga, an iron bar, transformed a struggle of ragged urchins intent on filching a bag of sugar into a murder of barbarians. What short-circuitry flashed this image to the nightmare cesspool of memory where charring corpses twist in the flames of rubber tyres and mobs of schoolchildren dance in rabid glee through the spiralling black palls of smoke? The fact is, the dog brought me none of these images. The fact is, the dog brings me only the same straggle of ragged, snot-nosed piccanins that has trailed me throughout my life, hovering on the periphery of consciousness like a cloud of midges, a straggle indistinguishable from the tattered barefoot urchins waiting cup-handed outside the cinemas and restaurants at night, outside the supermarkets, the silent groups that descended from nowhere on picnics in the countryside, the dusty packs that swung gates open at rural cattle-grids and scrabbled for my butt-ends, the squalid solemn groups of pot-bellied piccanins on the innocent farmlands of my childhood. The fact is, I swatted him like a fly, that boy – thoughtlessly, as one swats a fly, or tosses a coin, or flicks a butt-end out of the window. There's no psychopathy in that, is there – a reflexive swat of the hand? All this digging, Pretorius! Digging, digging, digging! A reflexive swat of the hand at the bothersome touch of a fly's wingtip: is that a total absence, or an absolute manifestation, of psychopathy? Put that way, is it not a moot point?

I am so tired. So tired. What answer can I give, my son, to the question that darkens your eyes? I have no answers. I am empty of meaning. Reflected on the profound black surface of your pupils my pale image floats like a ghost. I am weightless with exhaustion. Staring over the edge I feel as though I could fall down and down forever into those black craters. Perhaps I have always been there, on the edge, living astride a chasm of obliviousness, the immeasurable fissure of slow tectonic plates. I am a void of fatigue. I shut my eyes tight. Impaled on my pin of unknowing I pivot in nihility, watching the after-image of your dear eyes, my boy, growing strange, watching the fathomless dark lagoon of the pupil mutate in to a dead black face, the delicate rim of Raphael-blue iris raddle into a blooming nimbus of blood.

JOHN WAKEMAN

The Death of the Author

WEEK FIVE: It always turns them on, the Death of the Author. The obituaries still haven't reached the sixth forms, where Modernism rules embalmed, so Emma hears the news from my sculpt lips. She blushes.

At first they cannot believe their chewsome ears. They jib and shy and toss their manes. They stare at me, stunned or petulant. No one speaks, none cry out, but the exhausted air of the seminar room, hammered half to death by decades of flatus and afflatus, fizzes with unspoken questions. What author is dead? Dead how? How dead? All authors? My author? My Eliot, my Emily, my Blessed Sylvia Plath?

Because of course they're all booksy children here. Theologically bookstruck. Learning that *God* is dead, they've substituted Art – literature incarnate in some Great White Author or Toni Morrison. And here I am, in Week Five of Critical Theory and Practice, announcing the obsequies of that Fictional Supremo also.

It's a shock. It's a bereavement and Emma blushes.

Not Fat Emma, who has eyes only for haughty Francesca, and not Angry Emma with the snout ring, but *my* Emma, a prim slim sleeping beauty whose taut mouth and anxious eyes hint at sweet yearnings cruelly suppressed. She doesn't yet *know* that she is my Emma, but the guilty blush is rich in promise. There's masses of mileage in guilt.

I take it slowly. I stretch out my long legs and boyishly tip back my chair. I thrust my big hands into my pockets. Engagingly I blink into such wintry sunshine as seeps through the grimy windows. I scan the garland of variously troubled young faces. Mostly young.

'It's difficult, isn't it? It's *painful*. We're all trained to read literature, to study literature, to teach literature, in terms of its authors, the Promethean bringers of truth and light. And these are conveniently ordered for us into a hierarchy. Shakespeare at the top. Mills, say, & Boon, at the bottom. It might strike us occasionally that this arrangement is a touch arbitrary. Even vaguely undemocratic. But it used to be the only arrangement we had.'

We sit in a democratic circle of abridged high chairs, each with a little tray that can be cantilevered across in front of us to write on.

My tray is tucked back like an angel's wing because I have no need to write, but Emma is scratching furiously with a Parker pen on hers. She is inscribing in a hardbacked A4 volume many of my words forever. As she writes, a golden lock flops over a cornflower eye, is flipped impatiently back. As she writes, her pussycat tongue explores, more gently than mine will, her thin pink lips.

'What has changed is not the composition of the hierarchy. That has always been subject to the vagaries of fashion. What has happened is that the whole capitalist myth of a pantheon of cree-a-tors has simply gone out of the window.'

She glances up startled, from me to the window, then curls back over her book. She wriggles in her hard chair and crosses her Pretty Polly Bushfire legs, left over right, in the rust-coloured woollen skirt, which duly rides a little closer to glory.

'To understand how this has happened, we'll have to go back to the turn of the century. Back to the structural linguist Ferdinand de Saussure. Did all of you get to my Saussure lecture on Monday?'

I know, of course, which seven of them (besides dutiful Emma) had been there, which four had not. Poor Tony Fletcher vigorously nods his crooked head. There is a small babble of smug assent, incoherent apology.

'I can't *make* you go to lectures, but you're honestly very foolish if you don't.'

I glance at Daniel Tanner, an extravagantly mature student who never speaks in seminars, who had spurned my lecture, and whose presence in the university and the universe is a mystery to me.

'This is a case in point. There simply isn't enough seminar time to do justice to Saussure, but he's a crucial figure, the source of Structuralism. His work has transfigured not only linguistics but every other semiotic system, including literature.'

'What's semiotic?' asks Fat Emma, leering at Francesca for approval. Neither had attended my lecture, and would regret this when I marked their essays. Fat Emma would, anyway. Patrician Francesca is not without potential.

'Pertaining to signs and symbols as they are used in communication systems. Language is a semiotic system. Mathematics is. The Structuralists have shown that there are many such. Clothing is one: what we wear tells people who we think we are. Any others?'

'Semaphor,' says Tony Fletcher, as you might expect.

I like Tony. Whatever loathsome disease has withered his right arm and twisted his neck is said to cause him much distress. But he's cheerful with it, and respectful. The girls pet him, even Emma in her shy way. I don't mind. He's scarcely a threat.

'Back to Saussure. What did he say about language and thought?'

Tony waves his tendril arm. 'You can't think without language.'

'More or less. "Without language," he said, "thought is a vague, uncharted nebula, a shapeless and indistinct mass." Each language comprises a vast array of sounds and meanings, parts of speech, tenses and cases, grammatical rules and syntactical observances. The language is not any one of these things. It's not even *all* of these things. It is the whole web of their relationships, each to each, each to all.'

Some struggle with this, the light of intelligence flashing fitfully in their eyes like torches in a manhunt on a dark moor. Rather more sink glazed into the bogs.

'This structure, this infinitely complex fabric, is what orders and focuses our amorphous thought processes. It not only permits us to think, it governs *how* we think.'

Emma has stopped writing and is sucking the cap of her lucky Parker.

'Is that fairly clear so far?'

'It's clear, but it's not true.'

What? This from crumbly Daniel Tanner, in a high-pitched Cockney, rusty from disuse. Everyone looks at him as if he had risen from the dead.

'What?'

'Of course you can think without language.'

'Tell us about it, Daniel.'

The Death of the Author

He stares around the room, nods towards a metal table by the window.

'You could think about that table. Even without knowing it's called a table.'

We all look at the table. It's probably the first time in its career that it has borne such a weight of attention. That was a thought I had then about the table. Did I think that thought in words? Hard to say.

'It depends what you mean by thinking, Daniel. If you'd never seen a table before, you might nevertheless observe – well, let's say its flatness, and its height. Even without using either of those words, you might picture yourself having your dinner on it. Or a screw.'

There are giggles. (Daniel having a screw!)

'Certainly you could manage, more or less without language, "thinking" at that level of sophistication. But what if we want to go a bit further? Our mad scientists tell us that the table top is not really solid. It's actually a mass of whirling molecules that you could, theoretically, poke your finger through. I don't believe you could negotiate that concept without using language. Your certainly couldn't convey the concept to *others* without language. Could you?'

'Yes. You could go over to the table and shove your fist through it.'

Not faithful Emma, but two or three others, laugh at that, too. Tricky. Can't be seen to put the boot into a pathetic old git.

I throw back my head and guffaw full-throatedly along with the traitors. What has rattled Tanner's cage? He's a stocky old man with a steel wool crewcut. Sharp little piggy eyes in a deeply lined face like a dismal rocky landscape. Navy blue roll-neck sweater, Millett's cords.

He looks rather like Auden, who looked rather like my fascist terrible father.

'Nice answer Daniel,' I gurgle. 'Go on then. Show us how.'

He grins and shrugs, content with his little victory.

'No? shame. Now we'd better move on before I lose the thread entirely. Where were we? Emma?'

'Um. About whether you can, you know, think without words.'

'Exactly. And how that relates to the famous Death of the Author.'

I smile gratefully. Our eyes meet. I glance at my big old watch. 'Oh God, we're running out of time. Look, I'll just lay out the bones of the argument, and next week we'll put the meat on it. Just as well, because you'll have a chance to read the texts I've given you. Especially the Barthes please.'

'Now, whatever old Dan believes, we now know that our language is what permits and regulates our thinking. When we try to *communicate* our thoughts to others, we are clearly even more at the mercy of the language. Our thought, which is governed by the unique language structure we have inherited, can only be fully received by people who share that inheritance. And then only if we obey all of its laws and customs.'

'What about translations?' Tanner again, the bit between his hairy teeth.

'Big subject Dan. Save it for next week. Now, if the language *writes* the text, who decides its *meaning*?'

'The author,' avers the stubborn old fart.

'No. *I* do. *You* do. Each reader, at each reading, gives the text the only meaning it has. And this, as Barthes says, is what redeems the death of that sacred monster the author: the enthronement of the common reader.'

Oh they like it. They always do, once they get the hang of it. They love it, finding themselves the heroes of a bloodless revolution. Power to the People every time you crack a book. The Father dead at the turn of a page. They flash respectful glances at one another. They flash grateful glances at me. Emma does.

But Tanner is shaking his grizzly head.

'Hold on. What are you saying? I know that everyone . . . I mean, no two readers read exactly the same book. That's obvious. Everyone reads in the light of his own experience . . .'

'Or *her* own experience,' I say sharply. Always the ardent foe of male exclusivity.

'Yes. But it's silly to say that the author hasn't got anything to do with what the reader gets out of it, the novel or whatever it is. Of course he has.'

Snout-ring Emma turns on him like an enraged kitten.

'We *did* that. We did that in the New Critics. You're supposed to read the *text*, not the author.'

'Perhaps Danny disagrees with Wimsatt as well. Does anyone else?'

They turn their faces from Tanner, who studies the window. Someone's watch bleeps for four o'clock.

'Alright. Nobody late next Wednesday please. We have a lot to get through. And don't you *dare* to miss George Jekyll's lecture on the Russian Formalists. Seminal.' You have to say things like that when you're chairman of the Department.

As I pack my bag, my Emma approaches me. She is flushed in the throes of transference from the Dead Author to me.

'That was ever such a good seminar,' she blurts. 'Really . . . liberating.'

I drop a book and allow her to pick it up for me. The room has emptied. Our hands touch as I take the book from her.

'How's the essay going?'

'Um. I'm a bit stuck, really. Northrop Frye doesn't seem as close to Empson as I thought.'

'Well say so then. But look, if you could use some help, let's have a chat about it. I'm advising Monday mornings, ten to one, or . . . Tell you what, we're almost neighbours, aren't we?'

'I live just round the corner from you.'

'So drop in on Sunday evening. We'll look at a couple of texts, have a cup of tea, glass of wine. We'll be quite undisturbed.'

'That would be wonderful. But aren't you too busy to . . .?'

'Emma. It's what I'm in this university for.'

WEEK SEVEN: Daniel Tanner resists the Death of the Author because he is one. George Jekyll, his adviser, tells me that he is 'William Purchase', who writes Conradian adventure novels.

Purchase is one of those writers universally and perennially described as 'underrated', but he has some kind of coterie following. George has actually read some of his books, and admires them. But then, George is an unreconstructed Modernist who probably admires Conrad as well.

Tanner didn't show up last week, when we romped through Barthes, Foucault and Derrida, and still had fifteen minutes left for Feminist Criticism. (I had Angry Emma reading Hélène Cixous on the female orgasm as source of a truly female prose rhythm. Hilarious.)

Emma stole a proprietorial glance or two, but by and large was as good as gold. That turns out to be her problem. I am patient with her.

Today Tanner is back, sullen and unshaven. I don't anticipate problems with him this week. Theory has been left safely behind. We've moved on to Practical Criticism, cosily comparing the first page or so of *Persuasion*, *The Ambassadors* and 'In the Penal Settlement'.

As usual, most of them find Henry James opaque and the Kafka sick, but froth over Jane Austen. It will be my task to guide these young minds to a recognition that James's 'difficulty' is strategic. That Kafka's story about a clapped-out machine lethally inscribing their 'sentences' in the flesh of offenders is actually a Modernist attack on realism. Meanwhile I share their innocent enthusiasm for the breathtaking economy with which Austen lays her themes before us, the subtlety with which she etcetera.

'Jane Austen is an author,' chirps Tanner.

'That's right Dan,' I say warily.

'Last week – week before – you said the language writes the story and it's the reader who decides what it means.'

'That's what we're doing.'

'But this bit of *Persuasion*, we all think the same things about it.'

'As it happens.'

'*Not* as it happens. We all think exactly what she *wanted* us to think. You can't say it's the language that wrote the book. A person wrote it who'd got the language just where she wanted it.'

'You're taking all this much too literally Daniel. If you hadn't missed last week's seminar, when we dealt with Barthes' essay . . .'

'I *read* Barthes' essay. I stayed home and read everything he wrote. I think it's a con.'

'Go on then. Tell us why.'

'He's like all these critics we've been doing. He's trying to take over the literature, trying to bury the people that wrote it.'

Tanner leans forward, punching out words faster and faster in his vile accent. It occurs to me that he is drunk.

'All this guff about liberating the text from the tyranny of the author. Barthes doesn't liberate it. He *kidnaps* it. He locks it up and tortures it to death. Look at *The Pleasure of the Text*. Look what he does to Balzac in *S/Z*. That's *rape*. He pretends he's Robin Hood or something, handing literature over to the poor underprivileged reader. I'll tell you what he is really: the Marquis de Sade.'

Francesca laughs. I chuckle appreciatively.

'Very nice, Daniel. You have an essay there. But this is last week's work and we've got to move on . . .'

'You can't have it both ways. You can't have the author obliterated one week and analyzed the next. If the author is dead, if the author is irrelevant, what are we studying Jane Austen for? Why not your Mills & Boon? Why not the bloody telephone directory?'

'Why not indeed? Unfortunately, this department is still in the grip of the canon. Ha ha, you'd all be canon-fodder with me to rescue you.'

'So you really think a Mills & Boon is as good as Jane Austen? As good as *Shakespeare*?'

'Goodness, as Mae West remarked, has nothing to do with it. What do you think you mean by good?'

'I *know* what I mean by good. It's obvious. Shakespeare knows more about life than Mills and Boon. A hundred times more. And he says it a million times better.'

'That's the received wisdom. I don't happen to believe that literature has much to do with life, whatever *that* is. Except to the extent that both are linguistic phenomena.'

'Linguistic phenomena? *Life*? You ever seen a baby born? You ever seen a man killed? Linguistic my arse.'

'Please calm down, Daniel.'

'If you don't believe literature's got anything to do with life, if you don't believe life is even *real*, what are you teaching it for, what you fucking *living* for?'

He jabs his thick shaking finger at me, his geological face purple. Tony is staring at him with his face screwed up. Emma is studying the floor as Mother did when Father raged. No one helps me. None is loyal or ever has been. My eyes fill with tears. I cannot command them.

'You just shut up you drunken old fascist. Get out of my face.'

He lurches to his feet. I think he's going to hit me but he waddles past and flings open the door and goes. I close the door and sit down again and blow my nose. Silence. I draw some deep breaths.

'Oh dear. Sorry about that.'

I look at my watch, my trembling hand.

'I think we'll call it a day. He's obviously drunk, poor old guy. But let's just draw a veil over it, shall we? For his sake. I'll . . . I'll get it sorted.'

No one meets my eye, no one speaks, little shits. That's Emma's lot, she's had it.

'All essays in by next Wednesday. Any that aren't won't be marked. I shall accept no excuses.'

I pick up my bag and start out of the room. I turn back and collect some books from the arm of his chair: Svevo, *The Last of the Mohicans, Seven Types of Ambiguity*. I go along to the school office and ask the secretary for the number of Tanner's room. Is she a bit off-hand? Can he have been here? No. She finds what I want. Big smile for her Chairman, big smile back.

The numbering of the rooms in the concrete ziggurat where we sty our students is deliberately confusing, but I persevere until I find Tanner's.

He doesn't answer when I knock. I try the door and it opens and he's dead. He's lying on the bed with his mouth open and his eyes open, lit like a horror movie by the green glow from his word processor. Fucking mature students.

Inquest. Investigations. Publicity. Gossip. They can't pin anything on me but. One's chair recedes a little. Thank you very much.

The Death of the Author

The old Amstrad displays the end of a story. He must have been fiddling with it when he was taken ill. I run it back to the beginning. More Calvino than Conrad. We'd taught him something.

The story is called 'Last Words'. It's about a randy and arrogant lecturer in a provincial university. A critic and failed writer, he teaches literature but secretly hates and fears it.

Alone in his flat he tortures books. He burns them with cigarettes, staples their pages together, perforates them with his Black and Decker, boils them in his chip fryer. He clips *A Doll's House* into chains of paper dolls. *The Faerie Queene* he spraypaints with gross representations of Princess Diana's pudendum. He plays his recording of *King Lear* at the wrong speed, and wipes his arse on *Paradise Lost*.

He develops a skin disease that the doctors cannot identify. Patches of skin go paper white. Lines of ineradicable words appear on them, passages from the books he has tormented. As he moves, they writhe in endless intertextuality.

At first only his torso is affected and the quotations are easily concealed, though his busy sex-life is ended. Like a stick of rock, his penis reads *Ulysses* all the way through. Shakespeare's sonnets 86 and 129 arrive on his palms, which thereafter have to be gloved.

At last the word 'the' blinds his left eye, 'end' the right. He turns his face to the wall and dies. The University has him embalmed to preside naked at its annual literary luncheon.

I press *EXIT, ENTER* to call up the Menu, then f6, *ENTER* to erase. The text disappears as if it had never been.

Who is dead? Not the critic.

Biographies

JUDGES

Selima Hill was winner of the Arvon/International Observer Poetry Competition in 1989 and a judge in 1993. Other awards include a Cholmondeley Award for Literature, an Arts Council Writers Bursary, the University of East Anglia Writers Fellowship, and Poetry Book Society Recommendations for her books *Saying Hello at the Station* and *Trembling Hearts in the Bodies of Dogs*. She has read and taught nationally and internationally for many years, and currently tutors a masterclass at Exeter and Devon Arts Centre. Her sixth collection, *Violet*, is due to be published by Bloodaxe in 1997. She is married with three children and lives in Dorset.

Alexis Lykiard, Athens-born is now Exeter-based. At 17, won first Open English Scholarship to King's College, Cambridge, graduating with First Class Hons. Freelanced ever since. Several writing fellowships and residencies; tutor for Arvon Foundation and others since 1970s. Publishers' reader, reviewer and books editor. Nine published novels, including his first bestseller, *The Summer Ghosts*,1964. Many poetry collections – *Living Jazz*; *Cat Kin*, Sinclair-Stevenson, 1994 and, forthcoming, *Omnibus Occasions* with Headlock, 1996. Translator of numerous French authors.

CONTRIBUTORS

David Almond was born in Felling-on-Tyne, lives in Newcastle. Short stories widely published, and broadcast on Radio 4. Several prizes/awards. First short story collection, *Sleepless Nights*, published by Iron Press. Edited the fiction magazine, *Panurge*, 1987–93. Regular writing tutor at the Arvon Foundation, also for the Open College of the Arts. Is writing second novel and a sequence of linked stories which includes 'The Time Machine'. Other stories

Biographies

are forthcoming in *London Magazine*, *Northern Stories 6*, *Sunk Island Review*, *Panurge* and *Iron*.

Frances Angela is in her 40s, and lives in London with her partner and their son. She has worked in mental health and as a photographer.

Alex Barr has taught and practised architecture and has been a journalist. Now writes full-time, with stories on BBC radio and in *Stand* and *Iron* magazines. Has had plays on radio and on the London fringe, including *Goats*, set in Orkney 5,000 years ago. His poetry collection, *Letting in the Carnival* was published in 1984 by Harry Chambers/Peterloo Poets. In 1981, won first prize in the Piccadilly Radio Children's Short Story Competition.

Phil Bowen was born in Liverpool in 1949, now living in North Devon. Has worked as a drama teacher and publican. Writing since 1990, with most recent publication, *The Professor's Boots* with Westwords. Edited *Things We Said Today* to be published by Stride in October, 1995. Has a full collection to be published by Stride in 1996 called *Variety's Hammer*.

J.L. Brooke was born in Birmingham, but spent the early part of his adult life working in Africa, Europe and South East Asia. Now works in Worcestershire with people with learning difficulties. Has lived for many years in Wyre Forest in the Severn Valley, where 'Lifesaving' is set. Has written mainly poetry but has turned to the short story; is currently completing his first novel.

David Brown lives in New Zealand. Studied at the Auckland University School of Fine Arts, and has worked at various jobs. In 1994, received a New Writers' Grant from the Arts Council of New Zealand, Toi Aotearoa, and is presently working on a collection of short stories.

David Callard is 45 years old, best known as literary biographer of enigmatic figures – *Pretty Good for a Woman: The Enigma of Evelyn*

Scott, Cape 1985, and *The Case of Anna Kavan*, Peter Owen 1992. Winner of 1993 Tom-Gallon Award for Short Fiction, 1994 Hawthornden Fellow, where *Take the 'A' Train* was completed.

William Campbell was born on the North East coast, and graduated in Maths and Physics from Leeds University. He 48, and divorced; works as a computer analyst. Joined Slough Writers Group five years ago, and has had articles published, a play produced and won local competitions. Works with an improvisation dance group performing his poems. In 1994, founded *Story Teller*, a quarterly magazine for aspiring writers part-funded by the local council. His winning story in this anthology is his first entry in the Bridport Competition.

Sarah Carr was born in Reigate in 1971 to two mildly eccentric parents who gave her an inescapably Catholic upbringing. Studied theology at Leeds University and is currently completing a Master's Degree at Manchester University. Has spent time living and working in a hostel for the homeless in Edinburgh. Enjoys writing in all its forms and wishes she painted more.

John Dick - n/a.

Stephen Duncan is a poet and sculptor. He studied at Wimbledon School of Art, with postgraduate study at the Royal Academy and the Accademia di Belle Arti in Rome. He received a Rome Award in sculpture in 1993 at the British School at Rome, where he began his current 'Arcadia' series of sculptures and poems. 'Arcadia' has been exhibited in Rome and in the UK. His poetry has appeared in many magazines, the Arts Council and PEN poetry anthologies, Peterloo Preview 1, and the Arvon/Observer Poetry Collection. In 1994, he was awarded an Arts Council Writers' Award, a 'special commendation' in the Arvon competition and second prize in the Jewish Quarterly National Poetry Competition. In 1995, he won fourth prize in the Cardiff International Poetry Competition. This year's is his second success with Bridport.

Biographies

Richard Griffiths was born in 1960 and moved house, school and job compulsively for thirty two years until he arrived in a one-horse town called Ware, which he now quite likes. He works as a freelance systems analyst. He started writing two years ago, came third in the 1994 Bridport story competition and has had a story accepted by *Iron* magazine.

John Gurney lectured on degree courses until 1985 and has since been writing full time. Has won many prizes, including first prize with Bridport in 1992 and was a prizewinner in the National Poetry Competition 1991, 1992 and 1993, in the Arvon/Observer Competition in 1988, Kent & East Sussex, 1993 and the National Autism Society Competition in 1993. Won the Hastings Poetry Festival competition in 1994. Recent publications have been *Coal*, Taxus Press, 1994, *Mr Eliot's Summer Honeymoon*, University of Salzburg Press, 1995 and *Observing Dr Freud*, also Salzburg and due out late 1995. In 1991, his verse play, *Anna* was broadcast by the BBC.

George Hobson is American, currently serving as a deacon at The American Cathedral in Paris. He and his wife moved to France in the mid-70s, where they were involved in grassroots ecumenical work with the Catholic and Reformed Churches. Later, in Oxford, he earned his doctorate in Systematic Theology in 1989. He taught philosophy for the European Division of the University of Maryland before taking up his present post. Has written poetry since the age of 13, and in the last ten years has devoted as much time as possible to it. In 1984, was invited by BBC Radio Oxford to read excerpts during the Lenten Season from a long poem, 'The Bells of Swettl'.

Blánaid McKinney was born in 1961 in County Fermanagh, Northern Ireland and educated at Queen's University, Belfast. She lectured part-time there in Political Science before working as a civil servant in London and, for the past five years, in Scotland.

Brian McManus was born in Glasgow in 1957. One of only a handful of police officers to go the full distance on the Lockerbie

Biographies

Air Disaster Investigation, he left the force soon afterwards. A brief spell of self-employment was curtailed by continuing ill-health and he currently spends his time at home with his wife and young family.

Sylvia Oldroyd was born in 1942. A primary school teacher for 16 years, she is now a housewife, married to poet and librarian, with one teenage son. Member of two poetry workshop groups in Winchester and takes part regularly in local readings.

Kevin Parry was born in 1951 in Umtata, Transkei, South Africa. Educated at Rhodes University and the University of South Africa, from which he has a BA in History and History of Art. Has lived in England since 1979, working as a self-employed retailer. Began writing fiction in 1994 and is working on a collection of stories.

Jo Pestel is Irish but has lived in Britain for more than half her life, now living in a little village in East Kent. Has a grown-up family, and began writing poetry about two years ago.

Sheenagh Pugh was born in 1950 and read languages at Bristol University. Lives in Cardiff with her husband and two children. Has worked as a civil servant, trade union branch organiser, freelance writer and translator and, currently, is a tutor in creative writing at the University of Glamorgan.

Peter Regent was born and lives in East Anglia. In 1985, he published *Laughing Pig*, a collection of short stories, with Robin Clark/Quartet. Other stories have appeared in British and overseas periodicals and anthologies; several have been broadcast by the BBC. He lives in Scotland, dividing his time between writing and making sculpture.

William Scammell has published seven books of poetry and a critical study of Keith Douglas. He won the National Poetry Competition in 1989.

Biographies

Adam Schwartzman came to England from South Africa in 1991, when he was 17. Spent a year at Charterhouse School, followed by a year working as an assistant at an Oxford prep school. Started writing poetry in 1992, and won a supplementary prize with Bridport that year.

Ron Smith, born in Vancouver in 1943, studied at the University of British Columbia, with postgraduate work in England at the University of Leeds. Now lives on Vancouver Island. Has been published in magazines in Australia, Canada, Jugoslavia and the United States, as well as in Britain. In 1974, founded the publishing house, Oolichan Books, and was publisher until 1994. Between 1987 and 1990, was Fiction Editor for Douglas & McIntyre, and edited award-winning books for other Canadian publishers. His fourth book, *Enchantment & Other Demons* was published in 1995.

Alison Spritzler-Rose is a short story writer and novelist. Her work has appeared in *The Observer*, *The Printer's Devil*, *The Erotic Print Society Review* and the VER Poets Prizewinners' Anthology. She lives in London.

John Wakeman is a writer and editor, married to a Canon of Norwich Cathedral. They have five children. Has published stories and poems in magazines and anthologies, most recently *God*, Serpent's Tail, 1992. He recently completed a novel, *Ticktack*, about the millionaire surrealist Edward James, which brought him two Eastern Arts bursaries and a Hawthornden Fellowship. He co-edits the poetry magazine *The Rialto*.

Nicola Waldron was born in Kent in 1965. She currently teaches and lives next to a noisy road in West Yorkshire: her mind is usually elsewhere.

Kearan Williams was born in 1960 and grew up in a village near Holywell, North Wales. She read English at King's College, Cambridge and now lives on the edge of the Cambridgeshire Fens,

Biographies

working as a librarian in Cambridge. Her first published work, apart from that in this anthology, appears in *Poetry Wales* in Autumn, 1995.

Tanya Winter was born in Hampshire in 1973 but has lived most of her life in Darlington. This summer she graduated from St Mary's University College, Strawberry Hill, with a Bachelor of Arts degree in English and Classical Studies.